For the
Love
of
Money

For the

Love

of

Money

Creating Your Personal Reality

Liane Rich

The information contained in this book is not intended as a substitute for professional advice. Neither the publisher nor the author is engaged in rendering professional advice to the reader. The intent of the author is only to offer information of a general nature to assist you in your quest for emotional and spiritual well-being. In the event you use any of the information in this book for yourself, the author and the publisher assume no responsibility for your actions.

Loving Light Books
Copyright © 2014 Liane Rich

All rights reserved. This book may not be copied or reproduced in whole or in part, or transmitted in any form whatsoever, without written permission from the publisher, except for brief passages for review purposes.

ISBN 13: 978-1-878480-30-9
ISBN 10: 1-878480-30-8

Loving Light Books
www.lovinglightbooks.com
Also Available at:
Amazon: www.amazon.com
Barnes & Noble: www.barnesandnoble.com

for Richard

"This will be a book educating you on the energy of money, and your own value and love of self as it affects the amount of money that you *allow* into your life."

Preface

You are one of the few who do not realize your origins. You do not know who you are and you do not realize fully how you create your own personal reality.

You are about to discover your true creative nature and this is a time of great change in your awareness. You are about to shift up to a whole new understanding of your inner workings, and this will lead to an awareness (on a conscious level) of your creative abilities.

Most of you are in a state of transformation which has been occurring gradually over a span of several years. This transformation is taking place on a global level as it is a time of shifting consciousness up out of a semi-conscious state. This entails great movement of energies and these energies lie deep within each individual on earth.

Most of you are *aware* of certain changes that have been taking place within the earth; however, you seem quite unaware of the shift of energy *within* each individual. This book is an attempt to allow you to *see* how you are part of the energy of absolutely everything and you have an effect on this energy that you are a part of. You move within energy, you contain energy and you are made up of energy.

You are created from energy and you send out energy from within your very being – out into the universe in which you live. This energy is alive and is creative by nature. This energy has the ability to shift the atoms that are contained in this material world that you live in. You might say that you are all alchemists. You have the ability to shift one thing into another simply by the power that is sent out from you.

You are at a place in your evolution where you are all waking up to the fact that you can and you do create the world that you live in.

You are on the verge of discovering the "gift" in being you! You – meaning the spirit/soul you. You are not simply a human being with powers. You are a spiritual being, and with that insight you will begin to raise your level of awareness, and you will begin to view your life and yourself as a whole new entity with a whole new perspective.

You are being drawn to this book by your *desire* to create greater wealth in your life. The hope is that you begin to *see* how you are so much more powerful than you had previously realized.

I wish you well on your path up out of unconsciousness and into the awareness of your true nature. You are about to begin a big shift up into awareness and this book is meant to assist you in this process.

God

Note from Liane

For those of you who are new to God's books and curious to know more about the source of this information, I have published a small book titled, *For the Love of God: An Introduction to God*. This small book will give you a great deal of insight into this voice that speaks to me and writes through me. *For the Love of God: An Introduction to God* also appears as the Introduction to our book titled, *The Book of Love*. Either book will give you greater insight into this voice and the source of this information.

In the back of this book you will find a brief description of my first encounter with the God voice as well as a full list of book titles. I am told that repetition is used as a teaching tool in these books. God uses repetition freely and says that's the fastest way to get through our judgmental, conscious mind to the subconscious.

I hand write (channel) each book and type them myself. There is no editing of this material, so you are reading the original version as it was channeled by me. I think of this information as God giving me my own personal answers and guiding me to a more fulfilling life.

I hope you enjoy reading this new material and that it may give you a small bit of guidance in creating a beautiful life for yourself.

In Gratitude and Love,
Liane

"There are many roads to wealth just as there are many ways to achieve any goal...."

Introduction

For most of your life you may have struggled to come to terms with how you live your life and maybe even with the amount of wealth in your life. If you are looking for a better way to live your personal life and to receive the gifts you so richly deserve, this book is for you.

You will find this book, and the others that I have channeled through Liane, to be most helpful in going "within" and getting acquainted with your own God-self. You are a creative being and you have a long history of creating without the knowledge and awareness that you are now gaining.

As you read this book please be aware of the fact that it is a teaching tool. You will be led gently to new ideas that will open your awareness, and allow you (the creative part of you) to begin to see how you may choose a new way in which to create your life – in order to draw wealth and health and happiness into your life. This information is not new; however, I may be saying it in a way that is new for you. I tend to repeat information in an effort to allow you to absorb it into your subconscious.

You are not the first to question reality and you are not the first to be so totally unaware of the fact that your thoughts and beliefs are actually running your life. You will learn in this book the meaning of wealth and you will learn how to value "you" – the infinite creator of your personal reality.

Please sit back and enjoy the ride as I guide you gently into your prosperous and happy new future.

"As I have stated, if you do not like yourself you will not wish to give yourself gifts……"

I am now going to guide you to use your own creative power....

First off I wish to tell you that you do not require changing your thoughts and your beliefs. What you do require is trust in life, and God, and in yourself. Trust that you are part of God and trust that you can create anything that you desire.

Let's start with money. You wish to be wealthy as you do not wish to suffer and you do not wish to struggle. Money is easily created if you trust yourself to have money and not allow its presence in your life to complicate your life. You may have huge amounts of money and not worry about your future, or you may have huge amounts of money and worry about everything from how people may want to be your friend now that you are rich to how you will protect your money from theft and other losses.

When you have great wealth you do not worry so much about the little things, now you worry about larger issues. On the day that you become wealthy, you will begin to see how great wealth is a gift, by allowing yourself to know that you can always create more. Once you *realize* how you are the creator of all that occurs in your life, you will find it easier to allow money to be just another gift and not so precious as you might believe. Great wealth is the gift you give to yourself when you want to reward yourself. It does not have to do with punishment unless you *use* your wealth to punish. Always use your money for good and for helping yourself and others. Do not use your money to hinder or to manipulate governments or people. Money becomes what you say it is. If you believe it is to be used to stop wars then that becomes its purpose. If you say it is to be used to cause wars, then that is its purpose.

Money is energy and it may be used as any other energy force. Just as you can use your own personal energy to heal yourself and others, you may use money to heal yourself and others. Do not be afraid of wealth and do not fear lack of wealth. Poverty is simply a state of being, in which you are creatively learning to support yourself and your family. If you have little in the way of financial stability, you begin to find creative ways to make it through life. You tend to work closer with your friends and loved ones, in order to meet the day to day needs of your life. You tend to give more of yourself to help others instead of hinder others. There is more of a feeling of being "together" in this struggle to survive.

You see this in your daily lives all the time. In times of calamity and chaos from storms and great tragedies you tend to come together and do what you can to assist in giving aid. This is not by accident! Many of you are actually programmed to be part of the "whole." On some level you actually "know" that you are "all one" and you know that you are only as strong as your weakest link. You are all cells in this giant body that is God, and you are just now becoming "aware" of this fact. You are literally part of one another and you are part of this giant force that is known as God. You are not so much part of God as you are God. You are this creative force that so many speak of and pray to. You are the creative force that draws all of your life to you, and money is simply part of this three-dimensional illusion. You have given this part a very big and very important role in your three-dimensional, material world; and so I am now going to address this part of your life, in an attempt to allow you to understand what it is that you are requesting when you pray for money.

Money is not love and money is not gratitude and money is not respect! Money is energy that is sometimes *used* to buy these. Money is often the bartering tool in marriage – if he is poor as dirt no one wants to marry him. If she is poor as dirt she usually wants up out of the dirt and will grab hold of a wealthy man and hold on for dear life. If he has low self-esteem he may throw his money-weight around in an effort to gain respect. She may find that spending money to "show off" her style and good taste gains her respect. This is all part of the game that you play here on earth.

Many of you will only associate with those who are at your own level on the money scale. You would not be caught dead shopping in a thrift store or looking bad to your rich contemporaries. You often are drawn to friendships with those who live in your same monetary status. On earth status has become very important and this is causing some of you problems. You may actually be pushing money and wealth away because you have great disdain for the wealthy and how they behave.

You are not going to learn to be wealthy if you continue to hate, despise, loath and mistrust the very wealthy. You hate them for the way they treat and belittle others, and this leads to great confusion for the "creative" energies within you. You are not going to become wealthy by disapproving of all that the wealthy stand for. Begin to love the wealthy and begin to love the "idea" of being wealthy. If you feel intimidated by great wealth, you are saying to the universe, "I am not good enough for this" and the universe will respond with, "Okay, I will not give you what you do not wish!"

The one and only time that you are unafraid of 'not' being taken-care-of, is when you are totally and completely in the moment. When you are completely immersed in the present it is not possible to worry or fret about any possible future event. Being present and focused in the moment known as "now," allows you to create from "now." You spend so much of your time running from, and hiding from, and judging your past, that you are literally poisoning the "now" with the past.

Once you can learn to stay in the "now" moment and allow the past to fall away, you will be giving yourself a very big gift. Your future is also being brought into the now. You create your future out of your thoughts, and a good deal of your thoughts are about your future and how it may affect you. Let your future go! Allow your future to be unknown to you. You spend hour upon hour thinking of ways to keep you safe and the best way to be safe is simply to "trust" that all is okay and you will be safe. I want you to begin to see yourself as safe and protected by spirit. I want you to believe that all is well, and you will begin to create a feeling within you that there is nothing to worry about. Begin to ask God, or the universe, or Saints, or whoever you pray to, to send you trust. Ask constantly to "know trust." In knowing trust you will begin to feel trust. If you "feel" trust you will feel that your life is moving into a bright and safe and loving future. I want you to create a beautiful loving future for yourself; and since time does not really exist, and we are all living in this illusion of time, it is best to work from where we are.

So, if you desire "trust" you will be allowing yourself to trust. Trust does not come easily to you, as you have been programmed by society and by parents and even by a world that is skeptical. "It is not safe to trust!" This is the motto the world lives by at this present moment. When you do not trust, you create mistrust and concern and worry. This will eventually lead to a fearful and fear-filled future. You are creating your future from the present mixed with the past. I want you to end this way of creating. I want you to "trust!" Do not worry. Do not fret. Do not be afraid. Trust that there is a higher power and a creative force that runs through your life. Trust that this part of you will serve you and assist you in your life's journey. Trust that you are part of something greater than just your human body and mind. Trust that there is a powerful force that runs through you that you are totally unaware of. Trust that you can and do create your own reality.

Right now a good deal of what you create is created from the unconscious but very, very strong parts of you. You are a creative being. You co-create with God, or spirit, or powerful energy that permeates absolutely everything and you have no idea that you do. You are creating every moment of every day with the thoughts that you think. You are also (and this is very important) creating with the energy that you send out into the world in which you live. You create from this energy and you do not even realize that you carry this energy. You are like a ticking time bomb and when your clock runs out you begin to explode in anger, or you break down in sorrow and depression, or you begin to anesthetize yourself with medication or alcohol. You are beginning to break down in greater numbers because this is a time of breaking down the old patterns and making way for the new.

The new way is now upon you. The new way is a way of transformation from one way of living and thinking and moving in the world, into a new way of moving and living in trust, and the awareness that you are part of everything and everything is part of you. You are part of a giant creative force that many of you call God. If you are God and you come from God and you carry God (soul) in you, how is it that you do not consciously *realize* this fact? How is it that you contain soul energy and you do not *realize* that you do? Could it be that you are an unconscious version of yourself, and could it be that you are at a turning point in becoming conscious and *aware* of your true nature?

Could it be that you do not know who you are because you are in your infancy as a species? Could it be that as you reach certain stages in your growth you will begin to transform into a more mature, adult version of yourself? Could it be that this was the plan all along and that you entered into life on earth with full awareness of this situation? Could it be that upon entering this three dimensional world you begin to lose your awareness and go unconscious of the truth of your nature and your being? Could it be that after arrival into the realms of matter you actually go deeper into unconsciousness, until you can get a good foothold in matter? Could it be that, once you have a good foothold, you begin to bring into *you* more awareness and more energy to shift you up and out of unconsciousness? And could it be that this is that moment in time *for* you?

Could it be that you are shifting up out of unconsciousness and taking on awareness, and beginning a type of transformation that will allow you to use your creative power and ability in a whole new way? Could it possibly be that you are at a tilting point and about to shift in a whole new direction? Could it be that this shift will allow you to live from *trust* with no fear of the future "what ifs" that you currently carry? What if your life is about to change for the better in a very big way? And what if that change starts with you letting go of everything you now hold on to? Doesn't that sound scary to you? In order to obtain the shift that will take you to a better life you must let go....

As you may have deduced, this book is not about how you actually love money. It is more about how you keep money from you and how you create scarcity in your life. If you become aware of your patterns, you are then more likely to change your patterns.

You do not allow money to freely flow into your lives. You allow yourself enough to sustain your life style and you struggle to keep the flow of wealth steady. You do not seem to *realize* that you control the flow by allowing it or by blocking it. Think of the flow of money as water coming from a faucet. The wider you open the handle, the more water comes through the faucet and to you. You have been turning on your faucet only slightly in an effort to control how your life evolves. Most of you need or require total control over your life in order to (as you believe) keep you safe. You do not wish pain and struggle and so you put up blocks to certain events and you refuse to risk loss. Loss is very painful to you and you will avoid it at all cost.

There are others who "push" everything away in an effort to stay safe. You believe that you are undeserving of love and so you put yourself down and do not allow yourself to receive any of the gifts of life. You live in total fear and judgment, and often you believe that others wish to harm you or to take advantage of you.

You may find yourself enthralled with conspiracy theories and negative thinking regarding those who are powerful and prosperous. What this says to the universe and to your world is, "let them fall from their high horse, they don't deserve all that money. They are bad; people with wealth are nasty and unloving and uncaring." Now, who in the world would wish to be part of this group of people? You have created a world, your own private little world, where wealthy, powerful, influential people are not only the enemy; they are someone to be feared.

So, if you hate being unloving and uncaring and a bully who abuses your power, you will not wish to be too rich. You must learn to let go of some of your ideas, thoughts and beliefs regarding the wealthy. Allow wealthy people and powerful people to be a good thing. Admire those who achieve their own successes. Do not tear them down with your thoughts. Allow those who hold great wealth to be loved and not feared. You will not draw great wealth to you as long as you label the wealthy as bad, or mean, or dishonest. This is due to the fact that you do not wish to be seen as bad, or mean, or dishonest.

It is all you, controlling your world and what you allow into your world. Let go of your need to control and begin to *allow* life to be good, and fun, and light. You may *choose* to see the world as a good, fun, lighthearted, magical place or you may choose to see the world as a big, scary, dark and dangerous place, full of bad people. You create the world you live in by the way you see it. The world is simply your mirror reflection of what is *in* you! You are projecting the conscious and unconscious energy that is inside of you out onto your world so that you might know you.

When you begin to change your thoughts and your beliefs and broaden them to *accept* all as good, you will begin to see how all is good.

It's all an illusion people! Give up the need to see danger and you will begin to see its opposite which is safety. You feel unsafe because you have become overprotective, and in some cases, very paranoid and now you are creating a world of fear for yourself. Your neighbor may begin to see love and freedom from fear and from danger, and that frightens you even more, so you *warn* them about the dangerous world out there and you warn your children and you instill fear wherever you can. These are the seeds that you plant year after year, and what you plant will grow into a garden and then a forest. Fear is taking over and giving you nervous energy, and you are literally a nervous species who locks and bolts your doors and takes medication "just in case" and buys insurance in preparation of the worst.

How in the world do you expect to give yourself the gift of wealth when you mistrust life so much? How can you give yourself a gift when you believe everything, including money, to be dangerous and cause problems? After all, "look at the Joneses, they became wealthy and then got a divorce. Look at the Smiths, they became wealthy and then became very snobbish." How in the world can you give yourself wealth when you have so many conflicting beliefs regarding wealth?

So what are we to do? I suggest you begin to "love." Love yourself and love them. Love everything in your life and allow it to continue to *flow* into your life. I do not mean romantically love all. I mean *accept*. Acceptance is what love is all about. Accept and "allow" the world to be a good and generous place, with no agenda to put you down or trick you or hurt you. Life is life! Life is energy. Life flows with nature. Life is affected by your thought energy. There are many variables at work here. This is a creative field that you live in. No one told you how you are a creator and so you have been running amuck with your creations. Let's get you back on track. Let's begin to create some gifts in your life. Let's switch from fear to love. This is the intent of this book. *For the Love of Money* could just as easily be titled *For the Love of Self*. This is good for now. I will write more tomorrow and I will bid you all a fond adieu!

❧❦❧

When you begin to see how having a fortune in money and wealth is actually a very good thing, you will no longer feel like you must speak in hushed tones regarding your wealth.

Most of you do not discuss money and if you do, you speak quietly and try not to offend anyone with your talk of finances. This is one subject on earth that is taboo. It is not polite to say, "I am so rich, and happy that I am!" Think about it. You can say that you have a new home and you love it. You can say that you have a big new truck and it is awesome. You can say that you have a great job that pays well. It is even okay to say that you are healthy and you have no health problems. It is not okay to say, "I am so rich that I am beside myself with joy!" It is considered vulgar and impolite and boastful and just plain rude.

How can you become something or attain something that, on a wide scale, is considered vulgar and rude? You spend your entire life working for money, and yet the world finds money offensive and unattractive on so many levels. This is the programming *in* you that must be set free and allowed to clear. You must come to a place where money makes you joyful and not fearful. You must come to a place where talk about money is not regarded as vulgar and rude. You must come to a place where money is love just as all in God's creation is love. *For the Love of Money* is being written to assist my channel in releasing her *subconscious beliefs* regarding money and wealth.

So, as you continue to delve into your beliefs surrounding money, you might want to take a look at some decisions that you may have made regarding money in your past lives. These decisions may be powerful and they may be affecting your present life in ways you do not understand. You all have underlying beliefs and patterns that affect you on a daily basis and you believe that you are simply being you. You are being you, and you are made up of a great deal of programming from your childhood on up to adulthood, and back as far as many past lives.

So, how do we let go of all the fears and phobias that we have picked up along the way regarding money? We begin by reprogramming ourselves with new insights and beliefs and awareness. Once we have reprogrammed ourselves we will be ready for the next step which is opening to receive. You see, you must be open to *receive* the gifts of creation or you will simply block your good when it arrives. Opening to receive entails loving the self to the extent that you *believe* you *deserve* all the gifts this world has to offer. It is good to be "open," it is good to "receive." Most of you push your good away in an effort to *protect* yourself.

You do not know how to love yourself and so you spend your life protecting yourself and fortifying your walls of protection, and you think this is love. Love is not protecting the self. Love is accepting and trusting the self. You do not trust you because you do not understand you. You do not understand certain parts of your nature and so you spend your time trying to control these parts. Once you learn to love you unconditionally you will be ready to obtain great wealth and continue to enjoy great wealth.

There are many roads to wealth just as there are many ways to achieve any goal. There is no one set way to do anything. You only need to desire it, create it, and open to *receive* it. Then you will want to continue the pattern in order to stay in the flow or vibration of wealth. You do not wish to lose it all after gaining it, so it's a good idea to continue to stay open and flexible with your love energy.

So, what is love energy? All energy vibrates and causes waves or sensations to move out from your core being. You are a vibrating, pulsing, creative being. You think you are human but you have actually become more spirit and a little less dense over time. So, this spirit that is you is creative in nature. It is God *in* you. You are literally part of God and God is very much a part of you.

So, this spirit that is in you is creative in nature and is also vibrating and sending out signals. Then you have your thoughts which pulse out from you and send signals. Next we have all that programming that you carry forth from lifetime after lifetime, and lastly we have all your childhood teachings from this lifetime. A lot of these childhood teachings were literally given to you by you. Say something occurred in your life when you were three years old. Maybe a chicken flew over your head and at that same moment it let go of its bowel contents and defecated on you. This could lead you to believe that big flying birds are dangerous and they do not like you. Maybe you got in trouble that same day for disobeying your parents. Your child's mind could decide that your parents have some kind of special power over nature or are working with nature to punish you for being disobedient.

We now have three-year-old-you believing that she is being punished by nature for her bad deed. She now has a locked-in belief that she is alone in this life and that her parents and nature are out to punish her at every turn. Now, as a grown adult, she may believe that she is alone in this world and that the world is out to get her.

It doesn't take much to program fear and mistrust of the world into the mind of a small child. This is only one small instance. You can imagine how many similar events have shaped your child's mind and how those thoughts and beliefs, created by the child in the moment, might affect the child's life and the way this child will respond to life. "Life is a dangerous place and we must protect ourselves at all costs" is strongly programmed into many of you. I am inviting you to let go of some of this unnecessary programming and begin to trust life once again by trusting "you." Trust that you are capable of flowing with life and trust that you are moving into a better life, and trust that the spirit you is taking real good care of you. Trust and acceptance vibrate much faster than mistrust and fear. Trust and acceptance scare you right now and you embrace mistrust and fear. As long as you embrace mistrust and fear you will send out signals and vibrations that draw greater mistrust and fear.

I would like you to begin to accept and to love and to trust. Trust you, trust life, trust God; trust that life is good. This will bring you out of fear and mistrust and will allow you to drop your huge need to protect yourself at all costs. This need to protect yourself is pushing life and love and money away from you. Vibrate love and acceptance and you will be sending out signals from you that say to the field of all possibilities that you are ready for more love and acceptance. Send out signals of mistrust and fear, and you will be saying to the field of all possibilities that you are ready for more fear and more mistrust.

You are a creative being! You create – that's what you do. You may change what you create by changing your vibration.

⁂

The first time that you began to use money, you were more than likely quite young. You may have been given a penny, a nickel, or a dime and told not to lose it. You may have felt like it was a big deal or you may not have understood what all the fuss was about. Later in life, as you developed an appreciation for money and all that it could buy, you may have squandered pennies and nickels and dimes. These coins are small and insignificant and you do not value them unless they are collectible pieces.

Once you learned the value of money you began to hang on to the large bills and put them in a safe place so as not to lose them. You still did not worry about pennies, nickels and dimes, as they were small and plentiful. If you lose a dime you do not worry, but if you lose a ten, twenty or fifty dollar bill you may be more concerned. Money is different in various countries but since my pen (my channel) lives in the United States, I will discuss United States currency; however you may apply this to any other currency such as yen, pounds and of course the euro.

So, as you learn the value of money, you begin to hold on to the larger bills and not worry so much about smaller bills. This is due to the *value* given to each piece of paper representing each bill. Once you get to larger bills such as fifties and one hundreds you are fairly careful not to lose or misplace those. The higher the number on the piece of paper, the greater your concern for that particular piece of paper. Why is this? Simply because this piece of paper is like an IOU that can be exchanged for goods and services. This piece of paper is like a gift certificate that is good for everything from food to housing. This piece of paper represents hours of work at the job of your choice.

Now, for some, this piece of paper represents fun and excitement. They make their money doing what they love and it's fun to make, so it's fun to spend. I want you to get to a place where you enjoy the *flow* of money and this will entail you seeing money differently. You will begin to see money as a gift and a pleasure in the same way that you see a flower or a tree as a gift and a pleasure. I want you to shift your perspective about money and begin to nurture it as you would nurture a plant or a collection of fine paintings, or a special gift or talent. Nurture and love money! Love is unconditional acceptance and I wish you to come to a place of unconditional acceptance with money. No longer will you disrespect it, disregard it or misplace it. You will begin to trade it wisely simply because it is valuable to you.

Right now you do not value your money. You curse not having enough of it and you sometimes *hide* what you do have. I want you to shift from hiding to valuing. Hiding your money is a way to keep it safe. Valuing your money is a way of making it grow. Whatever you *value* in your life you have respect for. If you value a painting or a prized plant you watch it, admire it, enjoy it and you love it. It has a place of value in your life and you do not squander it needlessly. You may exchange it for other valuable items or you may hold it in your possession just to *enjoy* having it.

Here is the truth about money. Money is paper. Most large bills are simply paper, however, this paper represents energy. This paper represents love and nurturing. You go to work day in and day out to make money so that you might feed and clothe yourself and your loved ones. You do this because you love them and you are learning to love yourself. Most of you do not enjoy the work that you do, but you *enjoy* making money. What if you began to enjoy the work? Maybe then the money would be more fun and less of a burden. There are many psychological issues "in" you regarding money and its role in your life. I want you to begin to enjoy money and not be afraid of losing money and never having more.

You will begin to move from a way of thinking about money into a new generous way of thinking about money. You will begin to trust that money is meant to flow to you just as all the gifts in life are meant to flow to you. When you begin to see and *receive* money differently, you will begin to *enjoy* the flow of money through your life on a daily basis. You will respect money and the value it brings to your life, and you will become *aware* of the various ways in which you use money to control others and, in doing so, you disrespect the value and purpose of your money.

This will be a book educating you on the energy of money, and your own value and love of self as it affects the amount of money that you *allow* into your life.

You will begin to understand your own beliefs and subconscious thoughts regarding money by simply asking yourself questions regarding money. Do I love money, yes or no? Do I relish the idea of having great wealth, yes or no? You may write questions regarding money and ask to receive your answers. You might write out a question, and then put your pen on the next line of your paper and wait for it to move. Sometimes your subconscious will write for you, and your part is simply to *allow* your pen to write whatever comes up for you.

If you choose, you may decide to have someone else ask you the questions and you answer them without *thinking* of an answer. Simply blurt out whatever comes to mind. As you continue to delve into your subconscious beliefs regarding money, you will begin to see how you may have some very strong feelings *in* you that are blocking your flow of financial wealth to you.

So, if you think you are going to be wealthy, you usually are. If you think you are going to have enough to just get by, you probably will. What you believe on a deep subconscious level affects you strongly and will cause you to draw to you, or block energy from you. If you are blocking, you will wish to "open" to receive. If you are blocking, you will be able to unblock at will. Often a personality who is blocking is a very protective personality. You may have formed ways of protecting yourself from life and from danger very early on, or even in past life.

So, to begin to unblock you, it is necessary to take off your armor and let down your walls of protection. You may do this gradually, as you have more than likely built these protective walls very gradually over time. As you begin, start small and work your way up to larger fear issues. You might begin by allowing someone into your life in a way you have never done before. Break one of your own rules regarding protection and allow the reins of your control to loosen. This is difficult for many of you simply because you do not wish to change and you do not wish to allow others to have free rein in your life. You want to be top dog and in control. You want to say what should or should not be done, and how it should or should not be done.

I am not asking you to change your behavior overnight. I am simply suggesting that if you wish to "open" to receive, you must "begin" to open. So, I do hope that you will enjoy this little process of opening yourself up to *trust*. Trust will bring you to a whole new level in your vibration. Trust allows energy to flow, and you are in great need of unblocking your flow and *allowing* the energy in you to move. Ride the wave to prosperity by allowing yourself to move with life and not be stuck in control and submerged in the denser energies of fear.

When you no longer feel the need for strict control you will begin to receive with gusto. Control is fear telling you that things can only go one way. Allow energy to move in all directions and you will be allowing you to receive from all directions. Right now you may be receiving from a small funnel of energy, but that will change when you "open" to receive greater flows of energy.

When you block the gifts of this world (meaning this energy world) you stifle the flow of energy to you. Say you receive a gift and it's expensive and you think it is ugly. Do not block the receiving of this gift by pushing it away. You might push it away by saying, "Oh, thank you, but I couldn't accept such an expensive gift." Or you might say, "No, this is not my style it's really too big for my home." Accept the gift graciously. Say, "Thank you so much for thinking of me," and mean it. Say, "Oh wow! I didn't know I was about to receive such a great gift!" This opens the door for energy to flow into you. This allows you to receive the next gift and the next. After you have received this once unwanted but now accepted gift, you may then pass it on to another who might enjoy it. Keep the flow of energy moving. Giving is receiving for someone else and you are all connected, so when you give to them you are actually receiving also.

Once you begin to "accept" all the good things that flow into your life, you will see how you are drawing more and more gifts to you. Money will soon be a big part of this gifting process. Do not turn down or push away money that is gifted to you! Some of you say you cannot be bought and I am not talking about bartering here. I am talking about those who wish to give you money as a gift with no expectation of return. In these cases I wish you to say, "Thank you; how nice of you!" Just as you would if someone gave you a box of chocolates or a new pair of shoes.

So, as you learn how to receive you will begin to find it fun and you will begin to enjoy this little game of give-and-take. If you are giving all the time you will wish to know that you may be trying to buy friends in order to keep them in your life. If your pattern is to control with your money, this is not give-and-take, this is control and manipulation. I wish you to learn how to trust life in such a way as to let go of your need for control and manipulation. Once you learn how you are creating absolutely everything that occurs in your life, you will begin to see how you wish to change a few things, and the first thing to do is to stop. Stop where you are and let the energies that you have been sending out into the world begin to slow down. After you stop and slow down your current way of controlling, you will be better equipped to begin the new flow of energy at the higher vibration you desire.

Not everything is coming to you at once, so it is necessary to unblock parts of you and, once they are working smoothly, we will work on unblocking other parts. Just remember that everything in creation is energy. Think of all the things you block and do not accept, and that will give you an idea of how blocked you are. Some of you do not block. You simply *allow* things to be what they are. This allows the energy to relax, simply because you are not pushing at it to be something other than what it is. "Live and let live" is a very good motto to live by. Do not judge life, as judgment is a most powerful energy and it is very, very dense. Judgment blocks the flow of energy to the extent that it can and does shut down the energy in your body. Judgment is best left alone. Do not entertain it and it will not entertain you. Think of life as a dance. You get to dance with whomever or whatever energy you choose. If you bring it into your life, it becomes a part of your life. Do not entertain judgment. Leave it alone.

For now I would like you to ask to see "trust" in your life and you will be opening the door to trust by doing so. Trust creates more trust just as mistrust creates greater mistrust. You get to decide how you see your world. No one can create in your world but you. How does your world look so far? Is it full of love and fun and light, or could it use a little lightening up? Lighten up on judgment and allow the world, your own personal view of the world, to be a good one!

You may begin to see how you do not wish to have wealth in your life due to the fact that you fear success. You fear being successful because you fear being on top. You want to go unnoticed because you do not wish to be held accountable for all the decisions that must be made once you are successful. If you become very wealthy you will be considered a great success and you may then be expected to perform as a success. You want to be left alone to be yourself and you do not see yourself as successful or admirable. You see yourself as more of a loser and a little unworthy of admiration and esteem. You see yourself as simple and ordinary and you see wealthy people as special. You do not view yourself as special and so you would be uncomfortable to have others make a fuss over you.

You will learn to see yourself as a little more deserving and a little higher in rank by raising your self-image and self-esteem. You are now regarding yourself with low self-esteem and this makes it difficult to give to the self. Once you raise your level of self-esteem you will be allowing yourself to *receive* more energy, simply because you will be liking and accepting your own self. When you like and accept your own self (or anyone else for that matter) you begin to give freely to you simply because you like you.

You don't often say to yourself, "Oh, I think I will give Joan a gift because I don't care for her very much." You do say, "Oh, I think I will give John a gift. I really like him." So, if you do not like or care for your own self, why in the world would you gift yourself? You gift others because you like them and you wish to reward them for their kindness to you, or you wish to make them happy. If you want to make them happy it may be that you are rewarding them in an attempt to receive some gratitude for yourself from them. Often people are grateful for the gifts they are given and they wish to thank you, and this will raise your own level of self-love and self-esteem. After all, it is very difficult to feel bad about yourself at the same moment that someone is thanking you for being wonderful.

So, we are dealing with self-esteem on a very large scale when we are accepting the energy of wealth. You are "giving" to you and the bigger part of you may not think that you deserve this big gift of unlimited financial abundance. It's a good idea to begin to nurture yourself and accept yourself in order to open yourself up to the "idea" that you are very good and lovable and likable and kind and just plain wonderful. Once you begin to see yourself as the wonderful person that you are, you will wish to give to yourself on a very big scale. Right now you may be a little closed down and closed off to the "idea" of success, simply because *more* is expected of the successful and you feel "less than" not more than.

So, as we continue to open up our own psyche to receive, we will wish to learn to raise our level of self-esteem. This may be done in several ways and I have actually written other books through this channel which may be helpful. This material, as all material that is read, is most effective when read more than once. Sometimes it is necessary to sneak information past the conscious critical mind in order to reach your subconscious where you carry storehouses of information and programming.

I am not asking you to push yourself to change. Each flower opens into full bloom at its own pace. Some are meant to open and others are not. Some are early bloomers and others are not. Please do not push others to see things your way. This only creates greater issues and problems on an energy level. Right now your inner workings and inner energy is so tangled up that it is necessary to ask you to stop rushing to and fro and simply breathe. Do not try to push your energy (your thoughts, your beliefs) on others. I want you to stop and slow your pace and allow your energy to relax. The energy "in" you is knotted up from years of decision-making and self-judgment and self-criticism. It's time to stop all of that and give yourself a much-needed break!

You will find that the best way to enter your

subconscious thoughts and beliefs regarding money is to begin to go *within* your own self. Many of you focus your attention on the world outside of you, when you actually create from the world inside of you. So, you want to connect with your inner realms and begin to learn what is *in* you and what makes you tick. This is easily enough accomplished once you have the *desire* set in place, in you, to access your inner workings.

Some of you will not enjoy this part of the process simply because you do not like yourself enough to explore your inner workings. Others do not enjoy finding anything that is considered to be negative about themselves, and still others will not wish to disturb any negative programming that is stored within the subconscious. Most of you spend your entire life running away from yourself, as you do not wish certain parts of you to be remembered. If you are one of these, you will find it difficult to explore the depths of your own psyche. Many have problems owning their own judgments, and have such a need to be seen as right and smart, that they will not wish to explore their own programming and inner workings.

There are many barriers that must be worked through to get to the energy *within* you that is actually making you tick and causing your creations. Creations come from strong belief and strong desire. The blocks to positive, lighter creations may come from denser, negative beliefs. Try to stay in the lighter more positive beliefs and thoughts. This will allow you to draw to you lighter more positive creations. The lighter you can be, the higher up you go in the vibrations you carry *within* you. The higher the vibration, the more you will draw to you that which is at the same vibration. It is all energy. The material plane is a plane of dense energy that may be moved and lifted to higher states. You live in a flexible world of matter and energy. You move energy by being *flexible* not by being *stuck* in a negative perspective or view of life. Change your perspective and you literally change your view.

Now, I could spend a lot of time explaining for you how to enter your own psyche and begin to change your programming. This subject is very powerful for you and will allow you the insight you require to *know your own self*. You will find that I have channeled an entire series of books on this subject and they are specifically designed to draw the reader "within" to his or her own center. If you care to read this series you will find them most fascinating and highly educational on the subject of creating your own personal reality. For now, I will simply tell you that you create the majority of your reality from stores of information that are buried within you. You are a vibrating, creative being and the information that is ruling your life is literally stored within every cell of your body. Your body is the storehouse of your creative energy.

Look down at your body. Do you treat it like a valuable, creative mechanism or do you push it around all day and simply expect it to do your bidding? Do you love it and nurture it or do you simply expect it to work for you day after day? Do you allow it to rest when it requires rest or do you drink a stimulant of caffeine and push it further? This is your creative machine. This is the oven that makes the cookies and other goodies in your life. Do you appreciate the fact that your body works for you physically and also allows you to work mentally? Without your body where would your mind be?

Do not be so harsh with your body. It creates your life. All of the cells of your body carry the information that makes you up. You have millions of years of information *within* you. It is all energy. It fits neatly within your cells. Your cells carry all that you are and have information *in* them. How do you think this book is being written? It is energy! It is soul energy within the cells. Everything is right inside of you! Treat *you* like a queen or a king. Your body is so important to you. It houses the cells which contain information that creates your entire life. Love your body. Appreciate your body. It works for you day and night. Do you say "thank you" or do you simply expect more?

※

You will begin to draw great gifts into your life by allowing yourself to be "worthy." Worthiness is different for each of you. Some may consider themselves unworthy because they believe themselves to be sinners. Shame is a very big block when it comes to receiving your good. If you carry large amounts of shame and guilt you will feel undeserving and unworthy of most gifts. Wealth, especially great wealth, is difficult to draw when the energy you carry is sending a signal into the world that says, "I require punishment, I have sinned."

When you begin to go "within" to examine the thoughts, beliefs and energies that you carry, you may discover a huge storage of guilt and shame. This guilt and shame must be dealt with if you wish to create and maintain great wealth. Otherwise, wealth may be achieved and received only to be squandered and lost. The loss of great wealth is common among lottery winners who do not know how to maintain wealth. So, if you wish to draw great wealth, I suggest you let go of these denser energies of shame and guilt. You will find that sin is not really sin, and forgiveness is the key to allowing the energy of shame and guilt to release and be on its way up and out of you.

Many of you have used lack and loss to punish yourself for years and this may be a very difficult pattern to let go of. The desire to punish is buried deep "within" you, but you may see signs of it within your personality. If you have a strong desire for self-punishment you will notice a *desire* to see others punished for their injustices. This is the most common telltale of your personality. Your desire to see them "get their just desserts" is simply a reflection out into your world showing you that the signal you are emitting into the world is, "I deserve punishment." This could be seen as simply, "send punishment" and so the universe does your bidding and sends lack and/or loss as a form of punishment, simply because you are a creative being and a master of the universe; so the universe/God/creative force does as you command.

When it comes to punishment there is also the option of loss and lack in the health department. You see, there really is no God judgment placed on you. God is neither a judge nor a facilitator of harsh punishment. Man creates, and God *allows* man his creations. Everything is energy and God is the creative energy that takes up all time and space. You might say that you live in a living field of energy and this energy is literally what makes you up. You *are* creative simply by nature of your being. Once you stop creating you are no longer alive. It is not possible to be energy and not be alive. After you have left your body you continue to create, however, your creations do not *appear* in material form.

So, as you create you take in energy and you release energy. All energy is meant to flow into you and out of you. You have found ways to block energy from entering and to hold on to energy that you do not wish to release. You have held on to guilt and judgment and self-criticism, and it is time to release these energies if you do not wish them to create for you. Whatever you carry in the way of energy does and will continue to affect your life. If you wish to draw wealth to you I suggest you let go of all shame, guilt, judgment and criticism. I am not suggesting that it is impossible to attain great wealth if you carry these energies. Anything is possible and anything you carry within you will have countless affects upon your life. This is just one way of creating positive energy in your life, which will allow you to stop blocking the flow of great gifts into your life.

Others may be extremely wealthy and may not be very positive and loving. This does not mean that they do not *deserve* wealth. Everyone is you and you are everyone. Maybe their beliefs are stronger in the area of "everyone deserving to have it all" and since you are them and they are you, they are creating great wealth because this belief is strongest "in" them. You will find your own way and you will achieve great wealth by removing your blocks to wealth first. This will allow you to flow and this will allow you to continue to receive, and this will allow you to stay fluid and in the "flow" of all good things including health.

Do not worry that you have too much to clear from your subconscious. It is not that big of a job to let go of shame and judgment and guilt. Each step of the way you will feel lighter and the energy "in" you will begin to shift. This is known as transformation and is being felt by many at this time. You have a great influx of enlightening information coming to you at this time. You live in the "information age" and much of this information is geared towards getting healthy both physically and mentally. You are being taught how to raise your thoughts in order to heal your life; and one of the benefits of healing is that your raise in vibration creates a shift in how you create and how energy flows *through* you. Energy is meant to move and to flow. Dense energy sitting in you will bog you down and block new lighter energy from moving into you. Unblock your flow by letting go of your belief in sin and punishment.

This is a very big one for you to accept since so many of you place such great store in the "idea" of sin. It is not true. No one sins against God. Sin is man's creation and has nothing to do with God. I have written an entire series of books on this subject and on the process of clearing and releasing the denser energies. This series is a must read if you are looking to go within and heal you from the inside out. I will list the titles for you in the back of this book.

For now, know that all is not lost. Know that you may unblock any blocks you currently carry that do not serve you. Know that you can open to receive great wealth and great health. Know that your desire to achieve great wealth has led you to this information; and with new insights into your own self you will be guided to assist your own self in achieving the gifts of this material plane. Everyone on the material plane is here to create as well as to bring light. You are achieving your goal. You are creating! Now we will assist you in creating on a whole new level!

The one and only reason you do not wish to have great wealth is fear. Fear of wealth and the subsequent lifestyle that it can afford is something that many of you fear. You do not wish the hassle of trying to figure out if your friends are in love with you for you or for your money. You would prefer to have a simple life where you know how you stand in their eyes. When you add money (especially lots of money) to the mix it gets a little more difficult to know if their affection for you is true or motivated by possible financial gain.

So, if you are unsure of how you will be received for your wealth, you may hesitate to go there. You may find it difficult to accept friendships and you may already feel that everyone is only out for what they can get. If they are out for what they can get, they will love you for what you can give to them. This is a form of objectification where one is only valued for the gifts or even the talents he can bring to the table. Most of you do not consciously *realize* that you carry these beliefs around money but they are a very big part of you. You do not wish to be used and objectified and this does affect how wealthy you may allow yourself to become.

So, if you have great fear of being used and maybe even *abused*, this will affect the amount of wealth that you allow yourself to have and to maintain. If you have been used in the past, as a child or as an adult, this will be affecting you. Some are "used" for labor purposes by friends and relatives. Some are used by parents who don't have an appreciation for children and their purpose in life. Often people are used by bosses and by authority figures who are simply ignorant to the needs of others, due to their own overpowering need to rise to the top of the corporate ladder and maintain control over the masses.

All fear-based energy has an effect on you and on how your energy is projected out from you. You are like a giant magnet that draws to you that which you contain. If you contain great stores of pain from past wounds to your psyche, you will more than likely be drawing more pain into your life. This could be in the form of health problems, relationship problems, or any other type of loss or lack that will cause you to struggle through life. I do not tell you this to make you sad or depressed about your life. I tell you this to shed a little light on how you create your life, so that you might decide to let go of the old way of creating and begin to open to a whole new way of creating a most abundant future for yourself.

Each step of the way will be a little more rewarding than the last. You will gradually begin to see areas where you do not trust, and this will allow you to change your thoughts and beliefs in each area. Once you begin to see the world and life as positive, you will be seeing your own reflection. You are always projecting your inner workings out onto the world you see. If you are carrying mostly positive energy *within* you, then you will be seeing a great deal of positive energy in the world around you. Energy makes up everything and you are also part of the energy of everything. You are interacting with energy every day, and you are part of the energy that you interact with.

I am not trying to get you to see how bad or wrong you are to create the way you create. I am simply trying to get you to see how you could give yourself so much more. There is no need to live in fear of loss. Live in joy of abundance and you will begin to see and feel abundant. You are not feeling abundant right now simply because the energy *in* you is drawing to you what you already are. We want to begin to "shift" up a level and become a more positive you. This will allow you to draw to you the more positive energies. As you draw a higher vibration of energy to you, you will begin to affect the energy field of your material world in a whole new way.

It all comes from "within" you! So it is best to begin to see what you carry "within" you. Once you become *aware* of what you carry in you, you will be in a better position to change what is in you to something that will assist you in your goal of drawing great wealth and abundance to you. The more you learn about yourself the greater your ability to project out lighter energy simply by changing your view of a situation from a negative view to a more passive view.

Now, I know this idea does not sit well with you. I am well aware of the fact that you are taught to stand up for your beliefs and to protest. I want you to stop all of that and simply "be." Simply flow with the energy of life for a while. Let go of your need to be so in control of everything and just float in the field of all possibilities. I am asking you to be passive until you can clear some of your harsher judgments that you carry. Judgment blocks the flow of good into your life. If you carry great stores of judgment "in" you, you are drawing more judgment into your life. Give judgment a break and become passive long enough to release some of these destructive judgment patterns. You will then be, a little softer and it will be easier for you to be flexible. Flexibility receives; judgment restricts and pushes away. Be flexible and be "open" to accept life and creation as it is. This will be you saying to the universe, "I am open and flexible and ready to *accept* my good!"

The only time you ask for financial assistance is when you need money and are low on funds. The ideal situation would be to ask for or desire money at all times.

You will learn that it is advantageous to desire money on a daily basis. If you wish to be financially wealthy begin to think of money as a gift that will continue to flow into your life. Do not ask for the universe to send you one million or two million or three million. Ask the universe for a steady flow of money into your life. This will allow you the opportunity to adjust to having steady money and it will allow you to gradually grow more and more prosperous. If you continue to see yourself receiving a big windfall and then it's over, you will receive and then it will stop. The trick here is to open a steady flow of money into your life.

This money may come from any source. Do not limit the source or sources that you might receive from. Some of you focus primarily on your job and do not allow for alternate sources of income. You get upset when you do not receive a raise and this is primarily due to the fact that you do not allow for another source of income. Allow all possibilities and begin to *trust* that money will always come to you from somewhere.

As you develop a stronger and stronger trust in the flow of money, I want you to *allow* for the flow of money out of your life. This is flow we are talking about. Money is energy and money moves into and out of your life. Keep the flow open and allow the flow in all directions. This is not a directive to go out and spend your money. This is a suggestion that you allow money to work for you. Do not hide your money and never look at or appreciate it. Also, do not throw your money away in reckless abandon. Do not allow debt to control your life. Learn to budget your income in such a way that you are using your financial wealth wisely. Know how much is available for spending and how much is available for saving and even how much is available for entertaining yourself.

Money is energy and all energy is God. God takes up all time and space and there really is nothing but God. This allows absolutely every living and non-living thing to be part of God. God is meant to be light energy and if you hold a positive image of God you will not have a problem seeing everything in the world as God. I have not discussed money thus far in my books as I have been preparing my channel to love herself and to overcome her fears regarding great wealth. God does not restrict his information to subjects that you feel are godlike. If you have read my other books you now understand how everything is God energy and how you are God energy. This information is the basis for working with energy and in creating a lighter reality.

So, if you do not think it appropriate that God is discussing money; I suggest you read my series titled *Loving Light Books* in an effort to open your closed and blocked areas. If you are blocked regarding wealth you will find it difficult to accept that God would speak so freely on this subject. Once you have read my series you will be more *open* to this information.

Now, for those of you who are still with me, I would like to discuss your bills. I would like you to begin to pay your bills with joy. When you receive your electric bill say, "Thank you. Thank you for providing me with much valued lights and television and other electrical service. I appreciate you allowing me to use electricity!" Something along these lines will do. I would like to see you pay your bills with love and gratitude.

This allows you to open to receive greater love and gratitude into your life. Love and gratitude are the two most powerful energies and I highly suggest that you use them often.

Once you are paying your bills with love and with gratitude I wish you to begin to spend your money with love and gratitude. Do not throw your money around and do not *waste* your wealth. When you spend out of control, you are disrespecting your financial situation; and disrespect will draw greater disrespect into your life. Live within your means and allow for your wealth to grow before you increase your spending habits. You often spend more than you realize and you often purchase items that you do not need and will never use. Hoarding is becoming a problem with some of you simply because you are so out of balance in this area.

Living in the material world and on the material plane has created some confusion and a great deal of mistrust for many of you. You are so afraid of not having enough that you hold on to absolutely everything. You even hold on to relationships that are not good for you and do not honor and show respect to you. I want you to begin to look at your patterns regarding material possessions. Can you let go of a few things to get the energy moving again in your life? Is there something you are holding tight to that is not allowing your life to move forward? What is it and can you or will you release it? What is the big fear "in" you that you believe will befall you if you do let go? Letting go is a very fast way to move forward and it will allow you to start the flow of energy moving in a very big way. You do not always see the results immediately but they will begin to shift you into a better position to receive.

For now, I would like to see you let go of a few things. Look at situations as well as relationships and material possessions. Let's get the energy "in" you moving so that you might begin to *shift* your energy "up" to the next level. You are energy. Get your energy up and moving. Allow the energy "in" you to shift by allowing you to let go in order to receive the flow of prosperity that is currently going around you, simply because you are too blocked-up to receive it.

The best thing for you to do if you wish to have great, unlimited wealth is to become unlimited in your behavior. You do not attract or draw unlimitedness to you by being limited. Once you have achieved limitless thinking, you will be creating with a limitless attitude. After all, the possibilities *are* limitless when you are God and you are creative in nature. The possibilities *are* limitless simply because you live in a field of limitless possibilities and potentiality!

How would it be to limit yourself when you are limitless? It would be like pretending to be human when you are actually spirit. Begin to live your life as though you are a spiritual being and you will begin to fulfill your true potential. You do not believe yourself to be spirit and so you continue to live and to create from a more limited perspective. Spirituality has a great deal more to do with how you create than it does with how well you understand your religion. Religion is a belief and it will affect your creations just as any belief that you hold on to affects how you create. Do not confuse creating and spirituality and religion.

Money is created by you for various reasons. Often you believe that you must agree to "give your wealth to help the poor" before God will allow you to receive great money. You make your agreements with God to give half away in order to receive. This constitutes belief in a limited God who will only share wealth with you if you are good and giving. This one belief is very powerful and is inside of many of you. Let this belief go! God is unlimited in giving as well as receiving. God is not stuck in an illusionary world as man is. God is not limited in how he sees creation. God is in man and man is in God, however, man is currently out of touch, or *communication,* with God. God has trouble getting through to man and communicating directly with man, as man is blocked and believes he is not connected to God. Man suffers because he does not consciously *know* himself.

This is about to change. The veil is being lifted and more and more of you will begin to reconnect with your own God-self. This is easier to accomplish once you begin to *accept* that absolutely anything is possible. Do not be so limited in your thinking as to believe that you are separate from the creative source of all energy. You come from within God and you are made up of God! Now, I have a reading assignment for you. I wish you to read our book titled *The Book of Love.* You are love energy and this book will begin to open your subconscious memory to this part of yourself. I channeled this book in an effort to explain the power of love in the simplest terms possible. My pen, as I like to call Liane, has a very simple vocabulary and is usually quite easy to understand. Repetitiveness and simplicity are what one requires if one is stuck in the complexities of what is going on within the field of matter.

You live *in* the material world yet you are a spirit and this fact has caused a few problems for you, but nothing that cannot be overcome. So, as you read *The Book of Love* I wish you to do any exercise that is suggested to get you to *open* to self-love. The more you love yourself the greater the chances become that you will wish to "give" to yourself. Once you begin to give to yourself you will be opening the flow of energy into you and you will be accepting you as good and wonderful. There is nothing quite like self-love. Self-love allows you to shift your vibration and this allows you to raise your own level of consciousness. You have been unconscious of who you are and how you create your world for some time, and now you are ready to see from a higher perspective. The more conscious you become the lighter and more flexible you become. After all, your goal here is to become conscious and to leave the unconscious state you now reside in.

This is the Grand Awakening! This is a time of waking up and raising the vibration of the entire world. This is a process that is being accessed by many at this time. The veil is being lifted so that you might see and understand how good and lovable you really are. You do not see yourselves as good and lovable and this causes your creations to be not so good and not so lovable. Love is key here! Love and gratitude are such strong energies and these two energies thrive and grow on *acceptance*. Acceptance is the key ingredient to making love and gratitude flourish. Accept yourself and you will be loving you. You do not accept yourself when you think, "I must be better than I am. I am not good enough. I am not smart enough. I am not talented enough." Any of the "not enough" thinking will draw "not enough" from the universe into your world and your life.

Be "enough." Be unlimited in your possibilities and be accepting of life and of yourself. Do not be so strict with yourself that you do not allow for joy and for self-love and for self-nurturing. You are growing and you are awakening to the fact that you are a creative force and you are not even aware of this fact!

The first time you break through your barriers to wealth you will begin to see how good it can be to give to yourself in this fashion. Most of you believe that to give to yourself is a selfish thing to do. There are also those who are so wrapped up in their fear of lack that they seldom think of others as a way of giving. If you are one of these it would be a good idea to begin to give to others in some way. After you learn how to do this you will be better at sharing. Sharing is kind of what it's all about. Sharing is the ability to assist others, and since you are all part of the same giant body, it would be a good place to start this giving energy moving in your life.

Then we have those who constantly give to others and do not believe that they themselves deserve. They will insist that you deserve, but allow themselves to be left out. This is quite common with mothers of children. Mothers often do for others to the extent that they lose their sense of self-importance. They literally feel less important than those they are nurturing and protecting from harm.

As you discover your patterns, I wish you to begin to give. Give to yourself if you are commonly giving to others, and give to others if you are most often giving to yourself. The idea here is to open the flow of wealth and not block it or close it off from any area of your life. Now, here's the tricky part when it comes to wealth, prosperity and abundance; they are all energy. Everything is energy. Giving is giving. Do you give love? Do you give support? Do you give kindness? Any of these will "open" energy pathways within you. If you give anger, criticism, guilt and judgment you block these same energy pathways. Keep this in mind. Love, kindness, gratitude and support lift-up and open-up. Anger, resentment, criticism, guilt and judgment push-down and close you down. Stay open! Be positive and allow your life to flow to you in uplifting and positive ways.

You are an energy creating machine. You create your life and you create the way you view it. Some of you have come into difficult circumstances from birth and this was set up ahead of time. You are acting out a role and you are learning to operate from within the material plane. You did not come into this world by accident. No one comes into this world by accident. Your spirit saw ahead of time how your life would look and was aware of "all" the possibilities this life held for you. Your spirit chose this life and even these parents. Your spirit knows you and has been here with you before. This is more than likely not your first go around in this material world.

Many of you actually have memories of some of your past lives and this is likely to assist you in this life. If you were very wealthy in a past life and you were treated unfairly, you may blame this on the fact that you had great wealth. Maybe you were used and manipulated by those who objectified you and wanted only to get their hands on your money. This may lead to a strong, *unconscious* desire in this lifetime to avoid great wealth. There are many variables at work within your subconscious, and these beliefs and patterns will affect you until you release them and take on new beliefs and patterns.

Self-talk is a good way of bringing your beliefs to the surface. You may want to use affirmations to assist in reprogramming yourself. Affirmations such as, "I am healthy and wealthy and I wish to continue with this good fortune" are very helpful. I have guided Liane to use subliminal recordings and these have been most helpful in allowing her to release some of her more negative self-judgments that were causing problems to her health. You will find recordings available for both affirmations and subliminal reprogramming and I highly recommend them. Whatever works for you, to change the patterns that are blocking the flow *in* you, will assist in *allowing* the flow of energy to move.

As you begin to open you up to new ideas and new positive energy, you will begin to see change in how you view your world. Any day of the week you may find people who see the world and the people in it as "going to hell in a handbasket." You may also find people who *view* the world as simply *changing* and growing in a new positive direction. It is all perspective, and your own personal perspective is based on the amount of fear or the amount of love that you carry. It is all within you. The world that you see is right inside of you and is simply being projected out of you and onto the screen of life!

When you begin to see how you have patterns within your own nature that are blocking the flow of wealth and prosperity into your life, you will make a choice as to whether you wish to keep these patterns in you or to let them go. It is best to allow any self-destructive pattern to go. One of the biggest blocks to the flow of energy into your life is fear of loss. Fear of loss causes you to "hold on" and to "manipulate" in ways you may not otherwise use. "Holding on" is easy enough to spot. You may not be able to let go of things out of fear you may need them, and you may not be able to let go of relationships out of fear of not having a particular person in your life.

Sometimes you are simply using people in the same way that you *use* things. You use things to make you look good to the outside world, and you may also use certain relationships to look good to the outside world. You want your family to look and act a certain way because you have come to believe that your family is somehow an extension of you. This causes you to fear how they are perceived and accepted in the world, and this also causes you to control and manipulate them to be the way you *think* they should be.

This is the number one cause of problems within relationships. One person is struggling to change another person into something that is a little more *acceptable*. This is when you know that you are not open and flexible in your thinking. If you were open and flexible, you would not contain this *need* to have everyone be *like* you in order to make you feel safe. You have fought many wars over your beliefs and your differences. This is not to say that you are wrong to have these fears and to control and manipulate in this way. Nothing is wrong and everything is simply energy and "cause and effect." If you do not wish to block the energy flow into your life I highly suggest that you open the areas in you that are blocked.

You may wish to start with trust. If you believe and trust that you will be taken care of by a smarter, more intelligent part of yourself, you might begin to let go of some of the fear that causes you to try to control every area of your life. This type of fear creates greater fear and draws to it greater concerns and worry. If you can let go and trust in one situation, it will be easier for you to let go and trust in the next situation. It is like a muscle that grows in strength the more you use it. This simple first letting go makes it easier to let go the next time, and then the time after that. Before you know it you will be flowing in areas you did not even realize you had. You will begin to feel like magic has come back into your life. You actually believed in magic when you were very small, but that soon changed as you were taught to fear life and the dangers of this world. You were taught to shut down and to close yourself off. You were told to be concerned about most things in life and so you trusted these teachings.

Now I come along and I tell you to trust and to open up to life, and you have all this programming in you that says the opposite. It will be very interesting to see what you choose to believe in, fear, or love and acceptance. Fear has been the golden god for many lifetimes now and it would be good to see you change and move in a new direction energetically. I hope you see the wisdom in letting go of fear and worry. You have your own reasons for all of your choices, and I just thought I would show you one more area where you might be blocking the flow of great gifts into your life.

※

As you begin to notice the parts of you that are blocking the flow of abundance, you will begin to see how you have been creating problems for you. Seeing brings awareness. When you are unaware you are unconscious. You are now becoming aware and this awareness will lead to greater recognition of all that you create. The goal here is to turn you into a conscious, aware creator. Right now you are unconscious of your ability to create.

So, as you discover new areas of blocks within, I wish you to allow time for these blocks to clear. Most of you want instant results and you do not allow for change. You want change but you are impatient when it comes to receiving the gifts of change. Once you do begin to receive change in the flow of energy to you, I wish you to remember that you are clearing blocks of tangled energy and this energy must rise to the surface in order to leave you. Sometimes the energy leaving is quite strong and it is magnetic in nature, as all energy within you is. You may draw more of this magnetic energy to you, since it is releasing within you and coming up to be cleared from your body.

You do not require further change at these times. What you do require is calm and patience. Be sure to allow yourself the time that is required to heal all wounded areas in you. You are the number one reason you do not allow yourself to have great unlimited wealth. You may have beliefs within you that require you to rest as you let go of these beliefs. It could be as simple as the belief that you are not as good as everyone else. If this is your predominant belief you will often compare yourself to your friends and neighbors, and you will see their lives and their situations as much better than your own. As you begin to release this type of low self-esteem you may feel it grow in you. If this energy is recognized and then released within you to clear your body, you will bring it to the forefront of your consciousness for clearing and it will draw "like" energy to it as it clears.

If you have been working on your awareness and your ability to create, do not be upset and give up when, or if, things get worse before they get better. Sometimes the best way to heal an infection is to bring it to the surface for release. There is powerful energy that has been trapped in your subconscious mind and this energy affects your life and all that you do. It even affects how you think and how you believe. Let it all go. Do not be afraid of energy. You are energy and you do not realize that you are. You are vibrating and moving in ways you do not realize. You are constantly sending out signals and you are totally unaware that you do. If you send the signals that say, "loss is great in my life" you will receive "loss is great in my life." Focus on what you want, not on what you don't want. If you want wealth, focus on how much you do have not how much you don't have. If you have a problem focusing on what you do have, it means there's an energy pathway that is blocked and this pathway needs to open.

Look for something to appreciate and give thanks for. If you find a dime celebrate your find. If someone gives you a flower celebrate the gift of receiving. If no one gives you a flower then give yourself a flower. Give; give; give. Giving is receiving. Give yourself a soak in a tub with soothing music playing. Give yourself a ride or a walk in the country and *allow* yourself to take the time to enjoy it. Give yourself the gift of patience and be sure to *allow* yourself to receive it. Stop pushing and controlling! You push yourself around all day long and you try to control the outcome of every event in your life. Let it go! Trust that life is good and trust that your soul will take you to a good and wonderful future.

Do not worry that you will fall flat on your face. When you are a child you know that falling down is part of the process. You get older and now you call a fall the end. It's not the end; it's not failure; it's just a fall. Learn to fall with grace and with dignity; a little humor would also be a good idea. Do not be so hard on yourself. You are literally beating yourself up with your own thoughts. Love you and nurture you, and your self-esteem will begin to soar. This is what is required to unblock your energy pathways. The simplest and quickest way to draw unlimited abundance into your life is to believe that you are good and you deserve it all. When you push yourself around all day and control who you are, you are objectifying you and you are *using* you to get the job done. When you are happy, you are working joyfully and you do not feel like a slave to your "fear of not having enough." When you are treating you with love and appreciation, you will begin to work from joy and you will be grateful for all the appreciation and love that is being heaped on you by you.

The first time you begin to see money flow into your life you will wish to jump for joy! Money can bring with it great joy. Money can also bring sorrow. The majority of you will experience joy and then fear. You will want the money flow to last forever and you may begin to fear that it will not. You do not wish to fear lack of money, as this will cause anxiety and stress. When you fear anything you begin to create energy around it. Fear is a very strong emotion and fear sends a strong signal that carries the thought that is behind the fear. In this case the thought behind the fear would be, "Oh no, the money is going to stop coming."

So now you have this thought out in the world creating for you and it is backed by strong emotions. The stronger the feeling behind a thought, the greater the potential for that thought to create, or to draw the thought energy to you. Once you begin to draw the energy to you, you will see how you were right all along. This is how you prove your rightness to the world. You begin to believe something and then you *draw* situations to you that will confirm your beliefs. You have done this for eons and in this way you, as a species, have convinced yourselves of many false truths. You believe something to be true simply because it was once proven to be true. It is not necessarily the truth. You change all the time and you live in a field of potentiality and you are made up of energy; and you create your world and your life as you grow in awareness, or as you sink deeper into unconsciousness.

Do not be afraid to come *up* out of mass consciousness. Do not be afraid to be different and do not be afraid of loss. The mass consciousness at this time is one of fear and you are taught to protect yourself and to hoard and to build walls of protection. This is about to change; and you are going to begin to move into conscious awareness of the fact that you are an energy being, and you create and draw life situations to you simply by the emotional thoughts that you send out from you.

Now, you may spend all your time sitting around trying to think up positive thoughts, or, you may choose to simply let go of the negative thoughts and beliefs that you carry. Get up each day with one goal in mind. That goal is to find something good to focus on for the day. Find a good thought or a positive saying. Find a good thing that you like and give thanks. This puts two major energies to work for you – love and gratitude.

Love, as I speak of it in this book, is simply acceptance. When you *accept,* you open the pathways to receive. You may begin with a simple positive statement such as, "I am happy, healthy and wealthy and I wish to continue with this good fortune." You may also go with something a little more dynamic like, "I am so rich – thank you God!" Either of these will raise your vibration for the day. A raised vibration draws to it a higher vibration in the way of manifestations.

You are beginning to see how it is very important to stay "up beat" and even "happy." Like attracts like in the world of energy and fear will attract greater fear. Guess what love (acceptance) attracts? You got it. Keep yourself in a loving place and you will receive lots of love. You may not see immediate results, but I assure you that love will be drawn to you. Do you want support in your life? Simply give others support and the energy of support will come back to you. Think of your thoughts as a boomerang – what goes out comes back. There are no enemies in the world. There is only you *creating* energy and drawing energy to you.

I have gone into great detail regarding this in past books but I wanted to share it with you once again. You see, repetition is a great teaching tool. The more I repeat something the greater the chance it will sink in and you will *receive* it. As you know by now, you are full of programming and a lot of your programming is ingrained in you, because you have repeatedly proved it to be true by sending out the same old signals (thoughts and beliefs) and drawing the same old energy to you. Now I want you to really let go of the fear that has created for you your entire life. Let go of fear and know that there is a higher energy and it will become your future. You are not so much stuck in a rut as you are stuck in fear. Fear will release when love comes in. Love and fear cannot live in the same space. Fear is dense and moves in a downward spiral of energy. Love is light and moves in an upward spiral of energy.

See everything through the eyes of love. Do not block the flow unless your *intent* is to continue to spiral down into the world of dense matter. This is a time of rising up to awareness and a much higher vibration. If you wish to change directions energetically and begin your rise up out of the denser energies, you will wish to let go of fear. "Not so easy to do!" – you say. Yes, I have seen you struggle with this dilemma lifetime after lifetime. I will ask you to simply *accept* any situation that comes into your life. In this way you will not be judging and fearing it. Simply accept it as containing something good until you begin to *see* the good. One of your problems is that you do not like change and so when change comes along you freak out. I want you to begin to embrace change. Know in the back of your mind that change is moving you into position for something new and good to appear in your life.

The reason you do not have great financial wealth at this time may also be a part of your lifetime plan. Some of you actually came into the world this lifetime with the intent to not acquire wealth. This is done for many reasons and the most common is to teach the ego to be humble. Humility is thought to be needed in order to love and appreciate life on this plane. Often the soul wishes to assist the personality in raising its vibration to love and acceptance. Once you have achieved love and acceptance, you will be able to live on the earth in total awareness of the fact that you are a spiritual being; and with that information comes great insight into the plan your soul may have set in place for you this lifetime.

You might say that you are a multi-level being and you are unaware of your many levels. You live from one perspective but you actually are creating on many levels. So, as you create from spirit you may be taken in a different direction. Spirit sees energy and spirit sees *all* of you. You see only one level of your nature. Think of yourself as a giant layered cake. All the layers of this cake are alive with energy, and all the layers send out energy signals into the atmosphere. The only problem is that you are focused only on your layer and the energy it sends out. What about the other layers of you? You are sending messages from all layers but you think you live in the top layer of the cake. Your energy is focused in the top layer and you think this is who you are.

Your spirit sees and is aware of all parts of you. Your spirit knows you require energy to move in a certain way for you to become untangled from any energy blocks that you contain. Your spirit is the aware and conscious part of you. You are the ego personality and, in most cases, you are afraid of anything you do not understand. One of the things you do not understand, and many do not accept and acknowledge, is the spirit world. You think you live in the material world of matter and that is all there is. What about the spirit world that you exist in? What about the other layers of you that you are unaware of? There is so much of you that you do not accept and own, simply because you are totally and completely unaware of these parts.

"What does this have to do with having great wealth?" – you ask. It is the basis of how you work in this three-dimensional world. Instead of seeing yourself as a cake with many layers of yourself that you are completely unaware of, I would like you to now take that image and see it as a body instead of a cake. This body has many parts that it is totally unaware of. It has hands and feet and fingers and toes. Only because this body is totally unaware of these parts it does not use these parts.

So here sits this body, and because it is unaware of its

own feet and toes it never knows it can walk and it never tries to walk. This body is unconscious of its ability to pick up a hammer and build a house because it does not know it has hands that can assist in building and creating. You have many parts of you that can assist in creating your life for you. These parts are basically unknown to you. You think there is only one way to create but there are actually many. One of the ways to create a good life is to send out trust and allow the spirit *in* you to do the work. I know that you have this saying that "God helps those who help themselves." This does work for many of you; however it is not the only way to create. I have asked Liane many times to sit and wait and I will deliver her good to her. She has difficulty with this type of patience, but over the years she has seen how God does provide for her and she has gotten much better at trusting that there is nothing to fear.

As we go along in this book, I want you to *realize* that there is *great* potential *within* you. You are multifaceted and multilayered and very powerful. You sometimes feel like a victim of this world because you do not understand how creation and creating works. None of this is punishment. There is no punishing God and you do not punish you! It is all energy. Energy draws to it more of the same energy. If you carry great stores of guilt you will draw punishment to you. Guilt says, "I am guilty." What happens in your world when someone is found guilty of something? A judge will sentence that person to a punishment. Some of you actually *believe* that you will be punished for your sins. You are a creative being who sends out signals into the universe. If your signal says, "I have sinned and deserve to be punished," you will be punished or *receive* punishment.

Stop sending these signals. Begin to forgive yourself for absolutely everything you have done in this lifetime. That will get the energy of forgiveness flowing in you and to you from the field of all possibilities, or the field of potentiality that you live in. Here's the trick: you are meant to be aware of the fact that you create by drawing energy to you. You are meant to wake up to the fact that you are a spirit living through a human form that was actually created by you the spirit. You are meant to wake up and *realize* that you are doing all of this.

   Right now you are so unconscious that it may take a bump on the head, or an accident, to wake you up enough that you want to explore your workings enough to get you to know how you work. Have you had a fall lately or a bump on the head? Have you felt like life is knocking you around in an attempt to get your attention? You create it all! The energy in you is telling you something and you are not even aware enough to hear. Listen to the signals that your life sends. Stop what you are currently doing and listen. Life has a way of communicating with you, as life is energy and you are energy. Do not judge you and do not judge life. Allow life to unfold before you and look for the gifts that are being offered. If you cannot see the gift in a situation I want you to sit calmly and not judge the situation. The gift will be revealed to you. Once you see the gift, hold on to it until you see your next gift. This will open the door to receiving for you. Some of you are so afraid of life that you do not receive a gift when it is sent to you. You must begin to see the gifts in your life in order to multiply the gifts.

You will continue to change as long as you are energy. Energy moves and merges with other energy. Energy is motion. It is constant motion. The more you change, the more you grow and expand in conscious awareness. You may not always enjoy the changes that take place for you; however, these changes are always taking you to the next level of awareness.

You can learn to accept change by allowing and accepting all that occurs in your life. Most often you fight against situations and this is a form of blocking the flow. As you open to allow and accept all situations, you will be *accepting* energy. Money *is* energy. When you block energy you could be blindly blocking the flow of wealth into your life. Say you were hurt in an accident and now you cannot perform your daily activities as easily as you once did. You may have become injured in such a way as to cause you pain every time you try to sit. You may have a back injury that does not allow you to sit at your work desk in comfort.

Because you cannot sit comfortably you get up to move around every hour. This leads to you moving and breathing and getting some stimulation each and every hour. After six months you return to your doctor for a checkup, and he tells you that you now have opened your circulatory system and your heart rate has improved and even your back is getting better. So, was the change good or was it bad? Maybe it was neither! Maybe the change was *acceptable*.

I want you to come to a place of acceptance and stop blocking the flow of energy into your life. I want you to *allow* life to unfold around you and for you. I want you to see life differently. I want you to see absolutely everything as a gift!

Once you learn to see everything as a gift, you will be receiving the gifts of this world with grace and with ease. Everything in life is meant to be received and accepted as part of life. You cannot receive just the things that you *think* are good and acceptable and still be *open*. When you are open you are wide open, and all the gifts of this life are available to you. Some of you close down, to the extent that you do not trust life and you do not trust God and you do not trust you! I want you to *open*, to the extent that you trust you enough to love you and let go of the fear that you carry regarding life in general. Let go of all mistrust and begin to see the good in life. This will bring you to a place where you will see only good and *allow* everything that occurs to be a good thing, even as you watch to see where the new energy is taking you. If you do not trust you, you are unable to trust life. Life is energy and if you block energy at every turn you will end up blocked! You are energy and you are blocking energy, and you are creating greater blocks *in* you as you do so.

Unblock you! Trust you! Trust life! Let go of your fear of life and of change. Change is all that can occur for you because change is what you really are. You are energy and energy moves and changes. *Allow* yourself to move and to change. Allow life to move and to change. This is what life is all about. You want to stop the energy, and redirect it and change it into what you can accept! I will tell you now that you are becoming so closed-off and shut-down, that you are demanding that everyone else behave the way *you* believe they should behave.

It is time to *allow* life to unfold in all its glory and beauty. This is done on a creative level and life will always flow. You are the one who is blocked and blocking. Let go! Go with the flow of life and all the struggle of life will end. Stop blocking the flow and you will *feel* the flow. You will no longer live in pain; you will live in peace and grace and joy and love. Struggle is caused by conflict. Some of you fight life to the very end; others accept life and death with grace and with a great deal of peace. Who do you think is happier in their life, the one who constantly pushes at life to change or the one who accepts life as it is?

I am not asking you to lie down and let life walk all over you. I am asking you to begin to *allow* life to change and grow in new directions. You can flow with life in any situation and not be hurt or harmed by life.

So, what does all this have to do with money? The more

you can accept and receive all energy, the more *open* you become; the more open you become, the more energy you receive. Wealth, health and joy are all energy. Energy moves to you just as the conveyor belt at the airport that brings your luggage to you. You pull off the bags you wish to keep and you let the others move on to those who want them. You do not need to *take* unwanted energy. It is possible, however, to allow energy to flow right through you and not stop it….

The reason you may not be wealthy has a great deal to do with trusting the process of life. Life is ebb and flow and give and take and constant movement. If you do not trust that life is constant and will always return to a stable state, you may disrupt this flow simply by blocking it.

The extent to which your life ebbs and flows is controlled by *you*. You stir the pot or control the energy movement of your own life. You require a certain amount of stimulus and so you fling your energy about to create this needed stimulus. Maybe you go out dancing or drinking or maybe you simply throw a party. You require given amounts of stimulus based on how energetic you are and sometimes based on how addicted you may or may not be. Stimulus requires you to move in a specific direction. When you are stimulated enough you will rest. At this point you will become calm and maybe even relaxed.

Relaxation is a very difficult state for many of you to achieve. You are so wound up and apprehensive about life that you fear being bored and you fear being too busy and, consequently, overwhelmed. If you can slow down and stop stirring the energy, you can and will achieve calm and relaxation. Some of you think you relax when you watch television but what you are really doing is *escaping*. Relaxation is achieved by calming the mind. Your mind is constantly going and trying to figure out how to achieve the next step in your life or the next step in your day. You all plan your days and sometimes your entire month or year. *This is control!* You do not know how to flow with life and you do not know how to "let go" and relax.

This is the state that I find you in and you are all asking for help in one area of your life or another. You are trapped in your own addictive patterns, and once you let go of these habits and addictions you will be free to "flow" and to "ebb" with life. So, if life is currently giving you all that you desire, I highly suggest you stay as you are and continue to create in this fashion. If, on the other hand, your life seems to be one long drama with big highs and lows, I highly suggest you stop stirring the pot.

I know that you don't believe you create your current situations, however, you do. You create it all. You are energy, and you move other energy and you draw to you energy that is directly related to the energy that you carry within your own body. You are a projector of energy and you affect the entire world! Stop stirring things up and *allow* your world to be one of peace and harmony and good health and prosperity for all. There is a way to do this, and in your near future you will begin to see more and more people who are *accepting* and *allowing* life to unfold, because they simply "trust" that life will bring them good things and life will treat them well.

You are the God of your life. You are the creative energy that came from God. You all believe that you are human and you contain a soul that came from God. The soul fills you up. It is in every cell in your body and every corner of you. You are a soul, a spirit. You are creative by nature, and you blame life for your creations or you blame God and it is all you!

You do not realize your own power and ability. Once we get you to *see*, really see, who and what you are, you will be amazed that it took so long for you to discover your own creative nature and ability. Some of you just think you are lucky or maybe you think that you have good karma. It is all you drawing your good to you. If you have been blocking your good, you will wish to go "within" and take a real good look at why you do not trust life to unfold naturally and to flow to you. Yes! You, my dear sweet child of God, are powerful enough to block the flow of life to you. You will wish to unblock and open up to receive!

The only time you do not wish to change is when you are in a state of fear. Fear blocks you from accepting any situation that is not what you wish. You mostly fear being harmed or any type of loss. Fear of loss has a great deal to do with how wealthy you may or may not become. Fear of loss is directly related to pain and suffering. You might say that the greater your fear of loss, the greater blocks you put up in order to keep danger and loss out of your life. You often hear of risk takers who make great amounts of money and this is one of the reasons.

As you let go of your need to protect yourself at all costs, you may find yourself a little more open to receive. I am not asking you to go out and take unnecessary financial risks. I am suggesting that you *open* to acceptance and begin to drop your self-protective impulses just a little. Some of you block thoughts and ideas before they have the opportunity to come to fruition. Some of you are so mistrusting that you don't allow anyone to share ideas with you. You think that you have all the best answers for you, and everyone else is simply wrong, or not like you. You are closed down, and if someone tries to suggest a new path for you, you simply block their point of view.

Once again I will caution you that I am not suggesting you start living your life for others. I am simply stating a fact, in an effort to show you how you might be blocking the flow of energy (and wealth) into your world or your life. As you continue to see how you block, you may acquire some insight in these areas of your life and stop this blocking process. You need not do what others suggest, but you may sit quietly and listen to their suggestions. You might then thank them for their ideas and tell them that you will think on it. This allows the energy to flow through you as opposed to blocking the energy which does not allow it into your reality.

Reality is a personal thing, and each individual lives and works within his or her own reality based on his or her beliefs. Each individual walks around believing they have the correct answers and anyone else is simply wrong if they have a different answer. *All of life on earth is simply a perception by each individual.* No one has the correct answers as there is no such thing. You will learn, in the distant future, that life on earth in this material plane is simply based on perception. If you see it a certain way then that is how you see the truth of your reality. If the person next to you sees it differently, from a perspective that is different from your own perspective, you may not agree with that person; however, you are not in control of his or her reality and you cannot change his or her reality.

When it comes to reality on planet earth, there really is no one reality. There are billions of realities all based on each individual's beliefs, thoughts and ideas. Perspective creates for you and my desire with this information is to raise you "up" to the next level of awareness so that your perspective might shift! As you shift your perspective you allow life and your *perception* of what reality is to shift and to expand. Expansion is the idea here. We want to get you to a level that is conducive to expansion and will allow you to grow in awareness which is light energy. When you block, you shut down and you literally go "down" in awareness. We are spiraling up to a higher level of consciousness in an effort to allow you to create greater wealth or prosperity. This includes all gifts of this world of creative energy – wealth of spirit as well as wealth of the material type.

Once you begin to accept ideas as energy, you will be able to "allow" ideas based on the ridiculous as well as ideas based on normal thought. The ridiculous to you may be normal for someone else. I am saying that it is a good idea to allow each individual his own ideas and thoughts and beliefs. I am saying that you can all get along and live peacefully together if you begin to allow others to have a different perspective, and to perceive life from a different point of view than yours.

As long as you continue to block ideas, thoughts and beliefs you will be blocking energy into your reality. Try to "allow" everything to be what it is without a desire to control it all. Allow the creative process of life to unfold and to deliver your good to you. "What if it doesn't deliver good" – you shout! It will deliver good if you allow it to. Good is inherent *in* you. If you believe life only delivers bad things to you I highly suggest you read our books titled *The Loving Light Books Series* (see "Introduction to the Loving Light Books Series" in the back of this book). This will allow you to begin to find the gift in every situation and to draw more gifts to you.

You do not require another how-to book so much as you require love. When you begin to love and to accept all as energy, you will see how energy is not dangerous. Energy can be used in dangerous ways but you are learning to trust and you will be opening up by trusting; and this will allow the energy within you to flow once again. When energy is all blocked up within you, it can cause a shutdown of the organs as well as a spiritual shut down. If you have been feeling alone and lost, I highly suggest you begin to open and accept life. Life is you. You are life. Your reality is solely based on your perception of who and what you are. What if you began to see yourself as a beautiful, creative being that had the *power* to create anything you wished for? You affect you! You affect your life! You are creating your life by your thoughts. Think trust! Trust you! Trust life! Trust… Trust… Trust….

❧

This is a time of great change on earth and within you. Each of you is beginning to feel the growth of self-awareness within your own being. You are becoming conscious. You will no longer create unconsciously and you will no longer sleep through life. This is the Grand Awakening and many are being guided to awaken to a greater awareness. This is the case with my pen. She is simply being told by her own inner guidance how to move forward in a more conscious enlightened way. As she puts pen to paper she is literally told information that will guide her to the next level in growth for herself. If you are reading this information you too are being guided to the next step in your evolution and your rise up out of unconsciousness.

Once you become clearer about how you are a creative force, you will begin to accept the possibility that you are indeed part of God; and that part of you that is God has the ability to use matter in such a way as to mold matter into life. You have the ability to create from your thoughts and to see life and the world as good and positive, or you may choose to see life and the world as negative. It is all a choice and you make this choice every second of every day. You choose by how you judge life and your world. You choose by how you *decide* to view each individual situation that occurs in life. You choose how you will observe each situation and how you will call it good or bad.

Each time that you label a situation as bad you cast one more brick onto the bad pile you are currently creating. Each time you choose to see one more situation as good, you toss one more brick onto the good pile. This continues until you have created a mountain of good or a mountain of bad. If bad outweighs or is greater than the good, you begin to view mostly bad in your life. When the good pile has outgrown the bad pile you are left to see mostly good in your life. You see what you have created, and then you sit around and discuss how awful life is or how good life is.

On certain subjects you do not yet have a point of view, because your vision of that subject has not been prejudiced by beliefs from past experience. If you do not have any pain around a particular subject from past experience, you will not *react* negatively to that experience. Once you have *decided* that the current situation is not good for whatever reason, you may then begin to build a mountain of bad around it. This continues through your lifetime until you are seeing huge mountains of good and bad in front of every situation. If the mountain is good you run towards that particular situation. If the mountain is bad you will avoid that situation at all costs.

Each situation is actually neutral before you judge it and toss it into one of your piles. I suggest that you begin to see it all as good, and your mountain of good will grow and begin to fill your entire life. This choice is yours. You may judge the situations in your life or you may accept and allow for the good to shine through. You have created these huge mountains and if the mountain is labeled "bad" it is blocking your good. Allow for neutral if you cannot call it good. If you do not see the good in a situation or event "leave it alone!" Do not judge it and do not give it the power to become "bad." You *choose* every day with every thought that you think.

You do not need to imagine your good if you do not create bad. If you simply *allow* everything to "be" it will not cause you problems. Do you want a problem-free life with little to no stress? Begin to choose *good*. You choose! You decide! You create your life because you are a creative being and creating is what you naturally do. No good. No bad. Just energy that is neutral please….

You will find that as you change the way you view the world you will be changing how you create your own personal reality. This will allow you to see more and more ways in which you draw situations and events into your life.

Say you decide to take a trip, and once you decide on your trip you discover that your finances are not sufficient to get you there and back again. Now you must decide how you will make this trip and where the money will come from. You decide to sell a couple prized possessions and this allows you to meet your financial goal. What you have just done sends a message out into the atmosphere. The message in this case is, "I want this trip so badly I will give up my prized possessions for it." The next time you have a choice between a trip or your possessions it will be easier to give up something in order to get something. You have established a path of energy that can (and in most cases will) build and grow. These pathways become roadways and then highways as they are used more and more by you during your life. They may actually become a pattern and a habit. What you now require is a *change* in your habits and patterns.

Try a new approach. The next time you require money

for something be patient. Trust that money will come in time for this needed and requested event. This is a process of waiting for your good to be delivered. You may be offered some money to housesit or water plants for a friend. You may pick up some extra cash washing cars or fixing your friends fence. You may even receive a check in the mail that you hadn't expected. Often you receive when you least expect it, and this is due to the fact that when you know money is coming your way you begin to plan what to do with it before it arrives, and this causes the energy to shift and you are literally spending the money before you have it. This is done on an energy level of course. You send the money back out into the ethers to pay your bills; by thinking of where you will spend it you create an energy pathway for it.

Do not plan in this manner. Think of receiving it and allow it to stay with you. You send energy out with your thoughts. You may choose to bring energy in with your thoughts. See you receiving money and see you having money and see everything in your life as being happy and well. See yourself as being a deserving person who is well taken care of. Trust that you will be taken care of and you will see a *shift* in the energy of your life. You are not here to suffer. You are here to create and to bring in light. Light is awareness and awareness allows you to lift yourself up out of unconsciousness. You are creating from an unconscious level and I wish to assist you in raising your level of awareness in order to help you. You want help or you would not continue to read this information. Trust is key here!

Your current world thrives on mistrust and a great deal of corruption. I want you to shift "up" to the next level which is trust and openness. You cannot be open and be corrupt. It does not work. Corruption requires secrecy, concealment and lies. Trust requires faith in oneself and in the creative force that surrounds you. You need not control and manipulate energy.

You literally exist in a field of potentiality. This entire field surrounds you and you are part of it. It is the creative force that you call God. You live inside of God and you are part of God. You contain God energy and you contain creative force. You are the creator of your reality and I will tell you now that your first step to attracting wealth to you is to believe that you are good and wonderful and awesome and very, very deserving.

You may contain love energy or you may contain judgment energy. Switch to love energy as "like attracts like" and if you contain self-love you will be attracting more love. Love receives, love does not struggle and block. Love receives and love gives out more of the same. You block the energy flow to you by pushing it away. Love does not block energy, fear blocks energy. Get aboard the love train, and trust that the direction it is taking you leads directly to trust and faith. Trust will allow you to have your hearts desire; judgment will push your hearts desire away.

When you judge others you are judging you. When you trust you there is no need to judge others. You have a ways to go before you get to self-awareness and the discovery that you are good and innocent and deserving. Now I will simply ask you to stop judgment and trust that everything is going to be okay. Stop struggling in your mind. Your mind creates your life for you and you require peace at this point in your evolution. Peace comes when you surrender to peace. Control and manipulation are your most used tools at this stage of the game. Control and manipulation will keep you tense and wound up and walking on eggshells your entire life. I want you to be relaxed and flowing and trusting. Sounds scary to you now, doesn't it? I want you to be relaxed and at peace and flowing *with* the energy field that you exist in. I want you to let go and trust. How far can you go? How will you do with this trust energy and where will it take you? You will never know if you do not try....

As you learn to *receive* from life you will be opening a new channel into your old awareness that will train you to "accept." Acceptance is fairly new to you, as you have been strongly guided and directed (by those who teach you) to not readily accept. You are taught to judge and to be a critical thinker and this blocks acceptance. To accept, you must "open" and to open, you must become vulnerable. You hate being vulnerable and you do not wish to show your vulnerability to anyone.

Vulnerability is considered a weakness and you are taught on earth to be strong and brave and to fight for what is right. Now I come to you and I say that the way to become powerful is to open up and be vulnerable. You more than likely will not even know how it feels to be vulnerable, as you have buried this part of yourself and you do not trust this part of you. You want to be strong and you want to keep your defensive line in place in order to "feel" strong. You are not so strong as you believe, and the walls of protection that you have erected all around you are crumbling from the energy that is being brought forward on earth at this time.

Your walls of protection are an illusion. It is a false sense of safety that you live behind in order to feel strong. You are not really strong, you are weak and you are very, very fragile in your current protective state. You are cracking and breaking at every turn. Each time someone criticizes you or disagrees with you, you begin to crack a little and this crack soon becomes a fracture and you are then blowing up at one another, then you are fighting and arguing. The next thing you know you feel wounded or hurt and it is all because you are not flexible.

You are stiff and crusty and you are breaking apart in many areas of your life. If you feel that your life is falling apart you just may be losing your protective shield. This hard crust, or shell that you live inside of, may be coming off and you may be losing the protection you so strongly desire.

When you desire something strongly enough you usually draw it into your life! You may not consciously *realize* that you desire safety; however, it is the main goal of many of you. "Safety from what?" – you ask. Safety from your own thoughts, beliefs and programming. You do not trust life and you live in a fear-filled world that you are afraid of. Inside of you is a very small vulnerable child who does not understand what life is about. You all ask to know what's really going on here and you all ask to know why you are here and even who you are. You do not understand from your current level of unconsciousness and lack of awareness how it all works. What is life all about? How do we get here? Why do we die? Where do we go when we die? Why is God punishing us and when will this madness stop so I can feel safe?

These are just some of the thoughts that plague you day in and day out. You don't know who you are and you don't know what your purpose in life is. You don't trust the powers that brought you into this world and you don't trust your own self. You only know what you know, and what you know has been taught to you by others who are just as afraid and mistrusting. They are trying to find their way, and they are procreating and bringing more spirits into this world of illusion, and passing on their fears to their young.

You are being taught to be strong and that only the strong survive. You are in constant fear of death and you do not know that you are. You all race about trying to build a nest for yourself and you provide what you call a nice little nest egg for your senior years; and you do not know that you are actually providing a way to protect yourself because you do not *believe* that you will be safe and taken care of. You spend your life trying to protect yourself and keep you safe and this sends out a message from you that says, "I don't trust that I am safe. I am in a state of danger. I must protect myself." This message is sent over and over again from *you*. It permeates the airways with energy that is coming from *within* you.

You wonder why you do not trust and cannot *accept* freely, and this is one of the reasons. It is not the complete problem but it has a very big impact on you and on how you behave in life. Are you afraid of life? Yes! For the most part you are. Can you learn to trust life? Yes, for the most part you can. Will you learn to trust life? Yes. If you continue on the path of self-discovery that you are now on, you will learn to trust life and yourself enough to set you free. Once you are free to be flexible you will see big changes in how you view life and receive life. Remember, you are a projector of energy. The beliefs, attitudes, judgments and thoughts that are programmed into you are all projected out onto the world that you see. If the energy is not "in" you then it cannot be projected out "onto" the world that you live in.

You are an energy being. You have the power "in" you to build an entire world that is conducive to peace and love and, not only tolerance, but total acceptance. You will see a "huge" shift in the world you are projecting out of you by allowing the fear that is "in" you to leave. This is often scary for you and sometimes this letting go of fear will make you feel vulnerable. Do not be afraid to feel your vulnerability. If you have been healing and moving in a direction that is more conducive to spirit, you may be clearing some of your fear energy. Spirit vibrates at a much higher rate than fear. Spirit is love energy and love is "acceptance." When you have acceptance running through you, you automatically let down your defenses and become vulnerable.

You will find that the greater your need to protect

yourself, the higher the chances are that fear is ruling your life. Energy attracts like energy. If you are full of fear you will attract more of the same. "Let go and let God" is a very good saying. If you cannot trust God then trust yourself or trust life. Find something to trust. Do not continue to put your trust in fear. Fear has been in control of your life for such a long time. Wouldn't you like to switch to love and allow acceptance to guide you. Allow life "in." Allow trust "in." Let go of the old way of viewing life through fear and come over to the new world view that is based in love and acceptance. No judgment please! Let the walls of protection fall away and begin to set your love free to create your life for you. What you send out is what you get back. Embrace life by accepting life, and life will return the energy to you by embracing and accepting you!

You will find that the best way to draw to you is to be calm and peaceful. When you are calm and peaceful, your energy *flows* from you in a smooth path. When you are upset and confused, your energy moves in all directions and is constantly changing directions. Your feelings may be jumping all over the spectrum and this creates and draws greater confusion to you.

If you wish to have a peace-filled, calm and beautiful life I highly suggest you only send out energy when you are peaceful and calm. How is this possible if you are a creative energy being who is always sending out energy? You will wish to learn to calm your thoughts and your feelings. This is why you are now in a state of confusion when it comes to love. You think love is asking for acceptance from another. What love really is, is accepting the self. Love of self is key in calming yourself. You do not need to frighten yourself further. You constantly frighten yourself with worries and fears. The need to worry is strongly programmed into you from your past experiences and teachers. This is a good time to let go of these types of programming, and begin to move up to a new calm and peaceful level of programming.

In the same way that you have been programmed to explode with negative emotions when you don't get your way, you may learn to stay calm and peaceful instead of explode. In the same way that you have been taught to worry and fret, you can be taught to trust and accept. One energy draws to you more fear and concern, the other energy draws to you greater love and peace. Do not fear a future that does not exist. You will be sending your energy into that future. Where your energy goes you eventually go. Begin to see positive outcomes to all your situations and always go to that thought-of-outcome. Leave worry behind you. Do not bring the worry from your past into your present moment. You create from this moment. You live in this moment and you project your past memories and fears onto the present. You then project future what-ifs and worries onto this present moment, and soon this current moment is loaded down with the energy of the past and of the future. You must begin each new day as a positive day and think only of positive outcomes.

Allow yourself to live a positive life by allowing yourself to live in the moment without putting the fear of life into your self. Give yourself a break and allow yourself to see only positive, peaceful outcomes to each situation you encounter. You create your life from the energy that you send out from you! Energy is not good or bad. It does not have a moral compass. Energy moves and changes as you move and change. The way to change the world that you see is to change your thinking. Think peace! Think love! Think acceptance! Think positive thoughts and trust the outcome.

Some of you have begun to watch your thoughts and train your mind. Then you act-out and cause a turn, or ripple effect, in the energy you send out. This is natural in the beginning. You are just now discovering "you." And *you* are quite complex and *you* are layered with many layers from childhood and back into past lives. These layers can and will be peeled away as you begin to change from a negative response to a positive response. The reason these layers will change as you change is simply because you are an energy being made up of layers of *thought energy*. This *thought energy* that makes you up can all be released and set free. When you hold on to strict beliefs about life and how it should or should not be, you create energy build-up, or what I like to call judgment build-up "in" you. You may release this energy build-up and allow new free-flowing pathways for energy, simply by changing your mind! Yes! It's just that easy…. Change your mind and you change everything. Change your mind and soon your entire life will begin to change.

Here's the problem for most of you – you do not wish to be seen as airy-fairy and foolish in your beliefs. You think that you maintain value if you continue to be a critical thinker. You are "afraid" to be different from the rest of your peers and you do not "trust" letting go of the status quo. And where has being part of the herd gotten you? Be different; think different and you will be creating from a whole new perspective. If you are currently moving in a direction you do not like, I highly suggest you begin to change how you think and believe. The choice is yours, you know? You may stay where you are and continue to create from fear and concern, or you may move into trust and a little faith that life is not so bad. Maybe, just maybe, life is what *you* make it into….

You will begin to learn new ways in which to draw wealth to you simply by your *desire* to be wealthy. Desire is a very powerful energy as is love and gratitude. Desire backed by love and gratitude will create powerful results for you. The most important ingredient is love. Love, or acceptance, is often lost in the equation but is the most important ingredient. As discussed previously, if you do not love, you do not accept; and if you do not accept, you put up barriers which cause the flow of good to you to actually go around you.

So, with strong desire, you may create an energy pathway directly to you, but the energy will flow around you if you have your walls of protection in place. So, how do we knock down these walls of protection? One way is to become vulnerable and to *allow* everything to be as it is. Once you can accept it as it is, it will begin to move in a way that is more conducive to your wishes, desires and dreams. Once energy is accepted "as is" it can then be shifted by desire into a more beautiful outcome. Say you receive the gift of a car and the car turns out to be a lemon. It looks really bad, you hate the color and the engine makes a very loud noise. Do you say "thank you" to God/the universe/yourself for delivering this car to you or do you say, "I don't want this it's junk!" It's best to say, "thank you" and let it be a gift. Allow everything that comes to you to be a gift. Do not block the flow.

Now, you do not need to keep this gift. It is important to *receive* it and be thankful for it. You may find that someone else is collecting this particular year of automobile, and when they see that you have it they will be most happy to make you a good offer on your thought-to-be lemon. This is a perfect example of you discovering gold and tossing it out because you do not *see* its true value. If you begin to accept everything that comes to you as a "gift" you will begin to "see" the lemons turn into possibilities. These are gifts flowing to you in disguise. You may also find that you receive a nice tax write off for donating used (and sometimes parts of) automobiles to charity. This has now turned your lemon into a little money and a gift for someone else.

Do not be so quick to reject the gifts you receive as not good enough. When you can learn to see the possibilities you then become flexible, and you are also opening the *flow* of energy into your life. Do not block the flow by judging it. It is a part of you that is delivering energy to you. You may find that the more open and accepting you can be, the more open and accepting you will become. As you open wider you will allow for greater energy to move into you. More is always what you seem to desire and yet, when you *receive* more, you are so busy judging it and rejecting it that you shut down your receptive channels, and you are all blocked-up and closed-off.

I would like you to open just a little. Become a little more grateful and a little less judgmental. If your attitude is one of mistrust, I would like you to open just a little and find something you can trust. Start small until you can open more. Trust that your child will be happy, or trust that your wife will be safe when she travels. Find one area where you would normally worry needlessly, and for just one day trust everything is going just as it should. Become the observer. This way you are spending an entire day sending the signal of "trust" out into the field of all possibilities. What you send out you get back, so this is like ordering "trust" to come back to you. This will give you an entire day off from ordering worry and fear to come back to you.

You get to choose the world that you live in, by the energy that you draw to you. After all, as the saying goes, "When life offers you lemons, make lemonade!"

We will begin to see great changes in our world once we begin to change the view, or the perspective, that we have of our world. This is true for your own personal world as well. Anything that you can do to bring joy into your own personal world will add joy energy to your global world.

Here is the problem with you changing – you do not wish to change! In most cases you are stuck in a rut of doing the same things in the same way. You do not realize that you are, but you do understand how "you like what you like and it's nobody's business except yours." This is a common thought pattern that goes out from you. If you could change this thought pattern to something more inclusive like, "I live my best life and I am willing to change for the better," we would begin to see some changes "for the better" in both your personal life and in the world around you. I know that most of you are so concerned about your own personal life and have little to no energy that you give to the rest of society. Here is the idea behind becoming a "willing to change you" kind of person. If you are willing to change, you are becoming flexible. Flexibility allows you to bend and to move with grace. Grace is most important for you as grace allows you to be part of nature and the rhythms of nature. You are blocking the flow to you, and you are creating an abrupt halt in the natural flow of energy by refusing to move out of your stubborn, set-in, habitual patterns.

Now, some habits are good and allow you to stay healthy and in good condition. Other habits are causing you problems, and these are the habits we are concerned with. You thought money was separate from nature and it is not. All creative energy is connected and is flowing within the same field of energy. If you wish to own a new car, it will come from the same field of energy as the gift of a new home, or a trip, or the gift of joy. When you request and *desire* joy, you begin to receive joy and this in turn allows you to change. "Change from what?" – you ask. Change from an energy path that has been drawing sadness to you. You begin to lose sadness by requesting, focusing on, and drawing joy to you.

If you begin to desire, focus on, and draw wealth to you, you will be creating *change*. If you do not like to change, it will be difficult to make the *change* to wealth. So, you may stick with who you are and how you are, or you may decide it's a good idea to embrace change. Most of you fear change to the extent that you avoid it at all costs. It is costing you. In some cases, your thoughts are so rigid that it will take a good jolt of energy to move you out of the rut that I call "this is who I am and I don't care what anyone else thinks!" When you decide to change, you will be moving "up" to a new level of awareness. You do not require a big change like uprooting your family and moving, so much as you require an attitude change. You require a "shift" in your thinking so that you are not controlling those around you with your personality. You require a shift that *allows* everyone to be who they are and allows you to be who you are.

You are not a "stuck in one position" being. You are a spirit who is moving and flowing with the creative force. You literally *are* creative force, so let yourself flow and move with the energy of your life. Do not hold on to your old ways so tightly. Do not be so stuck and set in your ways. Move with each new situation (that arises in your life) with grace and with ease. When you are moving with grace and with ease, life will flow *to you* with grace and with ease. When you are stuck in a rut, your energy is stuck and no new energy can flow *in* to you. Energy feeds you. You are an energy being. Do not block the flow. Allow energy to move and to circulate freely. Allow yourself to be broad-minded and accepting. Allow yourself to be a part of absolutely everything simply because you really are part of absolutely everything. Everything is constantly moving and changing and growing in awareness. This cannot be stopped. It is the natural evolution of energy. Energy moves and energy changes. Do not cripple your creative flow by refusing to flow with it!

You will begin to change when you grow weary of your present state of circumstances. Most of you live in your current state and you find it to be acceptable for you for now. Once you begin to question how you live and why you are here, things in your life begin to change. Questioning brings answers in the same way that acceptance brings solutions.

Once you can accept your current situation as something more than a punishment, you will be able to work within your current situation to change it. Not everyone is unhappy in life, and if you are one of the few who are truly joyful you will find yourself very, very glad to be alive. If you are unhappy, you may struggle to see the good in life. As you struggle, you create a current or pathway of struggle that becomes habitual. You begin to see everything and everyone struggling. As you grow in awareness and happiness, you begin to raise yourself up out of the struggle pattern and you begin to see how life can flow if you simply allow it to.

For those of you who feel that life is constantly kicking you around, I suggest that you find something acceptable about your current situation and focus only on it. Do not get into judgment and do not hate your life. You do not need to create pathways of hate and judgment flowing to you. Accept where you are until the energy calms down, and you then will be able to change the flow in a more positive direction. Once you are accepting it and allowing it to occur, you will be allowing it to run its course so that you might move forward with a more positive flow of energy coming to you. Once you have a more positive flow coming to you, you will raise your vibration just that much, and you will find that a higher vibration will bring a lighter life.

All life is made up of energy. The lighter the vibration the less density you draw to you. If you have been drawing the denser energies of struggle and dissatisfaction to you, you will wish to change "up" to trust and acceptance. Trust and acceptance will draw lighter energy to you than will judgment and resentment.

You must find your way out of struggle in order to allow wealth into your life. It is not always how you react; however, you do react to life as a long drawn out challenge, and I would like to see you react to life as a game. With a game, you are more apt to accept the challenge and see just how well you can do. With a game, you do not hate it if you don't always win. You *realize* that there are going to be ups and downs, and you are ready to accept them and to come out on the winning end. This is the kind of perspective you require in difficult situations in life. Know that your current situation will be changing, and *know* that you have a hand in changing it. Know that you can win this game that you play with yourself. Know that you are a spirit who inhabits a body, and you are here experiencing life *through* this human form. Know that the things you fear are not really harmful, and know that once you change your *perspective*, or shift your *view*, life changes and shifts also. This is all very simple once you get the hang of it. For now, I would like you to come up out of struggle. You can do this by shifting your energy from fighting against something to accepting, and by doing so you allow it to flow right on by.

How do you know that you are creating everything you see? If you see it a certain way you are "perceiving" it in that way. If you see it as bad and ugly, you are perceiving it as bad and ugly. Begin to see it as a possibility that may contain a fragment of good in it and you will begin to *shift* your perception of it.

Again I must mention that I am not suggesting you lay down your life to others and allow them to abuse you. I am simply suggesting that you have power in any situation, and you may have a highly charged situation that you may calm, by staying calm and perceiving it differently. If you do not wish to struggle, if you desire peace, you will find it. You always find what you are looking for, as you are the one who translates the energy of your life for you. Is it good or is it bad? How do you see it?

As you continue to see the value of change, you will continue to expand. Expansion is what it's all about. You are everything and you contain everything. You are part of the field of all possibilities and the field of all possibilities is part of you. You are literally the creative force at work in the material world of matter. You are spirit and you are made up of molecules and atoms, and you believe that you are worthless and insignificant. You judge yourself as not good enough and you do not see how truly magnificent you are.

As you learn to change and to be flexible, you will find that your life becomes easier and your life becomes more peaceful and calm. This is a direct result of your ability to *accept* and to "flow with" life. You are learning to flow with this field of possibilities that you exist within. When you flow with the field you are no longer fighting the flow, and therefore your struggles become fewer and your life becomes easier. You might say that you are learning to accept you. You are creative by nature, and this creativeness allows you to change anything within your current view of reality. You may change you and you may change your thoughts and you may change your beliefs. This allows you to become more acceptable to your own self.

As you change, you literally rewire the neurons in your brain and you create new connections for them. This allows you to establish a new way of thinking and believing. If your thoughts create your reality, don't you think it might be possible to rewire your own neurons to the extent that your beliefs change into a multi-purpose, multi-faceted, multi-generational acceptance of reality as a good, pure, divine event? What if reality were simply a projected image coming from you – from your own brain? What if you could change the image that you see simply by changing your mind? What if the only thing necessary for changing your mind were the ability to "let go" of your current belief model?

This is what I am asking you to do. "Let go" of all that you currently hold on to and allow for a new or expanded version of reality. Reality is subjective. Each individual lives and dies within their own personal reality. You hear stories of individuals who have amazing and unbelievable situations occur in their lives. Sometimes these situations are of the paranormal variety. You always find a way to disprove the paranormal if you are a very conservative thinker. Stay expansive. Stay broad-minded. *Allow* absolutely anything to be a possibility. You live in a field of all possibilities. Why are you accepting and allowing so little to be possible? Open up! Expand! Be a creative being by allowing yourself to be who and what you are. *Accept* this part of yourself and you will be accepting God the creator in you.

As you continue to grow and to move with the flow of your personal reality, you will find that your personal reality will begin to "shift" into a more flowing and accepting reality. It's just that simple – block the flow and you are fighting the flow by putting up roadblocks. Allow the flow and you are open to receive, and this struggle to survive ends.

Now, for those of you who believe in struggle and drama, you may wish to allow yourself to gain attention in another way. I do not say this lightly. It is important here to get you to see your patterns. Some of you love to fight and argue so you can *feel* like you are right and smart. This creates certain difficulties for you as you continue to prove to everyone else how wrong they are. This may not be your *intent*, however, for you to be right in an argument the other person must be made out to be wrong. The interesting part of this is that you live in your own individual reality that is simply a projection of your own mind. The opposing viewpoint is also coming from a personal reality that is being projected out onto the world.

None of it is real! You live in a field of *all* possibilities. All of it is possible! No one thing is real or not real. No one way is the truth of it. All ways are possible. When you begin to accept and to *allow* for all possibilities, you are *accepting* the field in which you exist to become part of you. You are allowing the magic of creation into you and therefore into your own personal reality. Open up! Expand! Allow absolutely everything and anything to become a possibility in your life. Your only problem in life is that you are unconscious, and once you wake up there will be light!

※

The more that you allow to occur in your life without fighting *against* it, the greater the opportunity for expansion. The greater the expansion the more energy you *allow* to flow to you and through you. Do not get caught up in the idea that everything must go your way. When you allow energy to flow to you, you may then begin to select the energy you wish to hold in highest regard. Right now you are so busy protecting yourself from things you don't want that you are becoming a wall of steel that everything simply reflects off of.

Allow yourself to see the gift in absolutely every situation and you will be allowing the energy to make it through your protective wall. Once you see a situation as bad for you, I want you to look at it and watch it with the knowledge that there is a gift in this situation. This gift may not be revealed to you at first glance but you will find it if you look. Simply stay calm and *observe* your situation. Do not rush to figure it all out at once. Sometimes the simple act of observing something literally changes the energy into something else. Remember, you are all creative beings and you have the ability to move and shift energy with your mind. Look at the situation and see the most desired outcome. If this sounds like hocus-pocus to you then I suggest you reread my previous writing concerning your expansion and broad mindedness.

If you are unable to see the good in a situation then I highly suggest that you move on. It is not a good idea to stay where you are not being regarded well. All situations cause change and often they cause you to grow and to expand. The more that you are able to grow and to expand, the better you will be at drawing higher vibrations to you. Higher vibrations are like gifts and rewards. The higher vibrations raise you "up" and allow you to "not sweat the small stuff," or, as I like to call it, "go with the flow."

So, as you allow these situations to become a possible good vibration, you will be opening up to a life of possible good vibrations. You will be tweaking you and adjusting you in an effort to change how you create. Think of yourself as a projector of sorts. Nothing that you see on the viewing screen of your life is real in that it is a projection, created by you to show you what you carry within you. If you see stupidity all around you it is an image that you are projecting. Why are you projecting this image of stupidity? Simply because you are judging everything as stupid. When you shift your "stupidity" judgment just a little and maybe start using "ignorance," or better yet, "unconsciousness" as your judgment call, you will then begin to project judgments or thoughts of unconsciousness out onto your world. Now you will be seeing a world that is unconscious, which carries a little less of a charge to it then judging the world as stupid.

You create it all. You are a creative being and you *project* your thoughts, your beliefs, and your judgments out onto the viewing screen of your life. If it is not inside of you, you will not see it projected onto your screen. Life is a mirror reflecting back to you. That which you see in the world around you, and the way that you *perceive* the world is coming from *you*. If you want to change the world change you!

You will discover that you will begin to draw to you a more conducive life filled with love and acceptance once you switch your thinking to love and acceptance.

So, how do you switch to love and acceptance when you have spent your whole life being critical and judgmental? This will not be easy for some of you, as you do not see yourselves as critical or judgmental. You think you have common sense and you think you are being a smart and discerning individual. You will not be caught looking foolish and you will not *accept* foolish behavior in your life. You are the epitome of common sense and you feel that you are working in a way that adds stability to your life. Most of you do not at all see how you are controlling and manipulating your life day in and day out. You think you have all the answers and yet you are searching for your answers. And what are the questions you search so diligently to answer? Number one question is, "How do I find love? Please send me love." Number two is, "How do I stay healthy?" And number three is, "How do I find and maintain wealth?"

If you know all the answers and you *believe* that the way you think and respond to life is the best way, why do you suppose you do not have perfect health and wealth and love in your life? If you are so sure that you have all the answers and you judge new ideas and new ways of seeing life, you just may get to stay where you are. You get to keep whatever you hold on to. Whatever you let go of will leave and be replaced by something else. So, why not let go of being how you now are and *allow* a new you to emerge? Could it be that you are "afraid" to not have control in your life? Could it be that your love of control is greater than your love of going with the universal flow? Could it be that you believe (deep within you) that life is not safe and you will not be safe if you do not struggle to maintain the walls of protection you have built?

It is time to let go of the old way of viewing life, and to do so one must *allow* a new way to come forward. You cannot *allow* a new way if you are so stuck in what you have now. If you are holding tightly to what you have now, you will not get to the next level. It is like climbing a ladder. If you wish to rise up to the next level you must take your foot off the bottom rung of the ladder and reach "up" for that next rung. You then place your foot down on the next step until it is time to lift it once again in midair and set it gently on the next rung. You are afraid to lift your foot up and you are psychologically stuck on the bottom rung of your ladder. You do not *trust* the feeling of having no place to put your foot down. You feel like you will fall if you do not keep both feet firmly on the ladder.

You are inadvertently keeping you grounded in an attempt to avoid falling off your ladder. You feel like there is great danger in falling and this is due to the fact that you do not trust! You do not trust you (the creative part of you). You do not trust life and you do not trust that you will achieve success and greatness in your life. Somewhere along the line you were taught that you cannot, or will not, achieve your goals. You can do this! You can learn to let go and trust this process. You can achieve great things and you can draw the best life has to offer to you.

You will learn that the greater you try, the greater you become at letting go. Start small. Let go of some pattern of behavior that is not too difficult for you to release. After you have let go and changed your thinking, and subsequently your feelings regarding this one subject, I wish you to move on and *accept* some other new and bold thought to embrace. As you continue to embrace these new, bold, expansive thoughts you will begin to let go of your closed-mindedness. As you let go of your closed-mindedness you become free to allow energy to move to you in new ways. It may take a while to direct your energy in a new way, but you do not require instant gratification unless you are very impatient. If you are very impatient you will be unable to expand easily. I suggest you calm yourself and learn to enjoy the flow of life.

This is my wish for you: I wish you begin to *allow* yourself to change! You want your life to change and yet *you* do not wish to change. Your life is but a mirror reflection of you. You are trying to change the image being projected onto the screen of your life. That image is coming from the projector (you). Change you! The image will then change.

As you continue to move towards a life of wealth, I wish you to keep in mind how you wish to spend your wealth. You do not wish to squander something that is valuable to you. Wealth is valuable to you and you will wish to allow it to become a most respected part of your life. Be grateful for your money in the same way that you are grateful for your most prized possessions. You will find that the more respect you give to your money the better off you will be. With respect you begin to receive a certain level of desire to keep money coming to you. When you do not respect something you literally push it away from you. Disrespect is actually a form of dislike, and disliking something is not wanting or not accepting it. If you do not *accept* it you will not receive it.

So, if you wish to increase the flow of money into your life I highly suggest that you begin to show a little respect for it. Respect is high regard set in motion. If you do not have high regard for money and have always been taught, or believed, that money is from bad people, or only used in bad ways, you may not feel too much respect for money itself. If your programming from your society tells you that rich people are in control and are using poor people to maintain that control, you may find it difficult to love and accept and respect the money that allowed these rich folks to be in control.

You may want to look at money from a whole new perspective in an effort to release your past programming and judgments towards money. If you have ever heard your parents argue over finances you may have developed a dislike of money early on. You may find that you have beliefs *in* you that tell you to "stay far away from money because it only causes problems." I will tell you now that money does not lead to problems. Fear of lack and fear of loss lead to issues around money; and fear of not being in control leads to issues around how money is used.

Money is not a problem unless *you* have made it into the cause of problems.

Many of you have this programming in you where you blame money for many problems including greed. Money is not a problem unless *you* believe that it is. If you believe that money is a problem, it then becomes a deficit instead of an asset in your personal reality. Your personal reality is where you live, and anything that is considered a problem in your personal reality is there simply because you are holding on to it and refuse to release it and allow it to become something positive. You get to choose what you decide to be problems in your own personal reality. You may find that there are many others who do not have an issue with the same ideas, or thoughts, or beliefs that you take issue with. This is due to the fact that they each live in their own personal reality, and they have decided to see it differently than you see it. Why? Maybe their life experiences have shown them something different from your life experiences. Maybe they see the gift, or the value, in things that you judge (out of your own personal fears) as not good or not safe or not valuable.

You each get to *decide* what you want to believe, and once you decide, you begin to build up energy around your choice to help keep you convinced that your way is the right way. I want you to begin to let go of the belief that there is a right way and a wrong way. There is *energy*. You turn energy into whatever you want it to be. At this time, in your evolution as a species, you are turning energy into fear. I want you to come out of fear and move into love and trust, and let go of fear. "Love is letting go of fear," and you can do this. You are capable of great change and you are capable of shifting and shaping energy into what you want to be, by the power of your thoughts. Begin to *think* positive, uplifting, embracing, highly flexible thoughts. Allow life to be good not bad. Allow you to be good not bad. Allow money to be good not bad.

The first time you begin to draw good things into your life I wish you to recognize the fact that you have created something wonderful for yourself. You must begin to *receive* gifts, and to receive gifts you must recognize them as such.

When you come from a place of wonder and amazement you are recognizing the magic that exists in your life. Wonder is a gift in itself. You live in a magical world in which you are the instructor. It is as though you are the leader of an orchestra, and simply by moving your magic wand the entire orchestra plays a soothing melody or a triumphant march. You are in control with a simple movement only you do not recognize this gift. You think there is noise and so you try to stop the noise of your life. You are creating the noise of your life by moving so fast. Slow it down and you will hear the melody of your life.

If you continue to create stress you will continue to hear noise. Stress is being created by you stretching yourself and pushing yourself to do more, to get more. There are also those of you who have sunk into depression and do not do much of anything. The joy, and the magic, has completely left you and you feel sad and miserable. You have lost your ability to create magic and, for the most part, no one believes in magic and miracles anymore. You have become too wise, too sophisticated in your thinking, and too narrow-minded to *accept* the concept of miracles and magic. So, what am I to do with you? How do I reach you when you are so shut down and closed off? I have contacted a few of you in the same way that I have contacted Liane. You are beginning to see more and more of you who are starting to wonder if there is something more than just the physical plane and the material world. Many of you are beginning to question what reality is and this is good.

As you continue to question and search for your answers, I want you to remember that you are a spirit living in a body. You are a creative being living in a world of matter. You are responsible for your world and your reality. You are projecting your world view and your reality in an effort to show you who you are, and to show you what you carry *within* you in the way of energy. If it is not *in* you, you will not see it reflected out onto the mirror that is your life. Your life is simply a reflection of all the joy, or pain, or love, or fear, or insecurity, or confusion that you carry *within* you. You may not like what you see, but I will guarantee you that if you hate what you see being reflected on your mirror, you are also hating that very part of you that is doing the projecting. If you see stupidity and you hate stupidity, you are hating the part of you that you judge as stupid.

It is all you! You are the creator of your reality and you are projecting your reality from the inside to the outside world. Learn to *accept* and embrace and love all parts of you. Whatever you hate in your world is coming from you. You cannot see someone else's projection. You see you; you do not see what is *in* them unless you are using them as your mirror!

You will begin to see how change can be your greatest ally. Change can lead you in a whole new direction energetically, and change can allow you to become a new person in some ways. Change is growth and you tend to see it only as something uncomfortable. If you can become comfortable with change you will live longer and healthier and happier lives.

Change allows the energy to merge with you and to continue to support you. You do not like change as you are set in your ways and you only "like what you like," and the rest you tend to shun.

When you shun life you are not accepting life and so life will boomerang "shunning" and "non-acceptance" right back to you. You will feel like you do not fit in and you will feel like you are not accepted, or maybe your ideas are not accepted by others. Why? Simply because you are shunning part of life, and so part of you is being shunned. Think of energy as an "order" that you send out. What you do and think and believe comes right back to you. Put out anger and resentment, and you will receive anger and resentment. Put out love and acceptance, and you will receive love and acceptance.

You are ordering your life experience each time that you send a powerful thought out from you. Thoughts have power and when you are really attached to a thought emotionally, that thought has even more power. This is why I constantly suggest that you "let go and let God," or "go with the flow." You are beginning to see the benefit in living your life in a calm and loving and peaceful way, and this is due to the fact that you are tired of being pushed and pulled by the energy that you send out.

So, once we get you to begin to *accept* change without consequently judging it as a bad thing, you will be sending a message out into the universe that says, "Maybe life is not so bad after all." Once you *shift* your thinking "up" to the "not so bad" level, you may then begin to gradually *receive* "not so bad" back. Then, as you learn to watch for the good in each and every situation, you will begin to see "good" and life will once again shift "up" to the next level of good. You are rising "up" as you learn and grow and change. This is often referred to as ascension, and it is also referred to as waking up to the fact that you can and will create heaven on earth!

Heaven on earth is not a fairytale. Heaven on earth is a possibility and a very likely occurrence, or projection, for each and every one of you. You create heaven on earth by shifting "up" from fear to love. Love is acceptance and love will draw to you all good things. Love will *allow* you to see the gifts so that you no longer unconsciously *block* the gifts life can, and often does, offer you. So, give love a chance and allow yourself to rise up out of fear of loss and lack, and even poverty. Come on "up" to heaven on earth and the fulfillment of all your dreams and desires. Stop blocking the flow of beauty into your life, by *allowing* life to be a miracle, and magical, and interesting, and fulfilling, and acceptable in every way.

How do you *see* your life today? How does your life look to you right now? Could it use a lift "up" and maybe some love and nurturing? Love your life and nurture your spiritual growth. Your spirit will allow you to become all that you can be. Spirit is waiting to assist you in your rise "up" out of the denser energies. Spirit is God and God is love. You have everything that you require to rise "up" to great heights and your full potential as a creative being. Do you want it? Will you accept change and allow change to move you "up" to the next level, and then again on to yet another level?

You are the creator of your life and *you*, my dear sweet child of God, are creating in the dark. Turn on the light of awareness *in* you by allowing you to change!

⁂

You will begin to see the greatest changes in yourself when you actually let go of your *need* to control life, and you allow everything to simply be what and how it is. You hate to give up control because you hate injustice and what you call the horrors of life. I will tell you now that the way to peace and love is in the letting go of war, and violence, and non-acceptance, and intolerance.

So, how intolerant are you? How much do you resent others and their ways? If you carry great intolerance inside of you, you will see intolerance reflected back to you. You are creating the world that you see by projecting it out onto your life, or your world. It does not have to be such a bad view of life coming to you. If you can just shift your attention and begin to look for the good in everything, your life view will change dramatically. Once you know how to find the good in any given situation, I wish you to *accept* the good that you have found and to remember it for the next time. Each time that you can shift your view from intolerance to tolerance, you have moved a little closer to heaven.

"What if someone were to break into your home and kill you" – you shout! I would suggest that you let go of such thoughts and begin instead to think thoughts of a more positive nature. Something like, "I am always safe and loved and supported by the universe and life," would be a good replacement thought. Do not be so concerned about "what ifs." You spend your entire life preparing for "what if" situations to occur and I wish you to change your "what ifs" to something like, "what if the world gives me great gifts?" "What if the world hands me wonderful opportunities at every turn?" "What if I live in health and wealth in my near future?" And, "what if I create love in my life instead of all this fear that I have been creating?"

Your thoughts and beliefs and fears are creating your world for you; allow your thoughts and beliefs to shift into a more positive outcome and you will see a more positive life. There are those of you who are handed great hardship and tragedy and you continue to maintain a positive outlook, and to receive positive energy in return. There are others who are handed tragedy and simply fall down under the weight of dense energy. You cannot seem to see your way out of certain situations, and you are consumed with worry and guilt and judgment, and the belief that life is harsh. Life is harsh if you choose to see it as such. Life is a joy and a pleasure if you choose instead to count your blessings and give thanks for any little positive thing you can find in your day. This giving thanks allows you to rise "up" just a little, and then the next "thank you" will get you a little more lighter until you are so light that you literally float, or flow with life. Once you get to the point of floating and flowing, you will know it. You will feel so good about your life and you will continue to look for the good stuff and allow the bad stuff to fall away.

You need not get involved with the energy that you do not wish to claim. Do not reject energy and do not push at it to go away. Energy will cling to you when you push at it. Why? Simply because you are holding it "in place" by pushing at it. Allow energy to flow right on by. Say you have a bad day and your thoughts are obsessive about the situation, or situations, that occurred. I do not suggest that you push your thoughts out of your mind. When you push at something it will persist and you will obsess until you feel the need to start a fight, or to argue, or to hit someone. Allow your thoughts to flow through you and sit calmly and observe them.

Your first instinct is usually to tell someone off when you are upset, and this only creates greater friction in your personal reality. If you can sit calmly and observe your thoughts, and even tell yourself that it's okay to have negative thoughts as long as you allow them to flow right by you, you will be releasing them. It is a good thing to release negative thoughts. Sometimes the situations which occur during your day are simply being created by old energy that you carry *in* you. Say you were abused or neglected as a child. You may have large stores of resentment and pain and anger deep *within* you.

You may have been holding this energy down in you for many years.

So, how do we get deep old hurts and wounds up and out of you, so that you might draw the lighter energies into your personal reality? We may require some sort of a trigger to get the old stuck-in-you pain energy to move. So, if you have been healing and changing and growing spiritually, you may find yourself healing some very deep old stuck-in-you wounds. And how do you heal something that is stuck in you like a giant thorn in your side? You bring it to the surface to be released.

If that thorn in your side is anger and resentment, you will wish to allow the energy of your wound to release. If you continue to push it away, you are actually pushing it deeper into your own self, because it is coming from your past and it lives *in* you.

Allow yourself to heal, by allowing and accepting that you are creating a better life for you by bringing your pain to the surface. Allow your pain's rising to the surface (so that you may release it) to be a very big gift! So, now you see how the difficult situation you had today was actually a trigger to get your pain moving "up" to the surface of you. Many of you carry old stuck-in-you wounds, and they are so stuck that they require a nudge to get them moving. They are like one of those old records that the needle would get stuck on, in your record player. You would have to nudge the needle to get it into the next groove; otherwise it played the same line of the song over and over again. You have been playing the same line over and over again. It is time for a nudge; and your situations are often set up by the fact that you are healing.

Once you begin to heal, you automatically begin to rise up to a higher level of awareness. This higher level of awareness allows you to raise up some of the denser energies that have found a home deep within you. You are cleaning house by healing. You are lifting yourself "up" to a much lighter vibration and this will allow you to begin to flow with life and to see the good in life.

When you are seeing the good in life it is because you are finally seeing from a cleaned-out you. You are the projector and what you carry *in* you is projected out onto your viewing screen of life. If you carry pain you see pain. If you carry joy, you see joy. Be thankful when you are triggered to release pain and do not judge it as something bad. You are releasing the energy that lives *in* you and this energy is leaving so that you might embrace love and a pain-free existence, and all that a pain-free existence might create for you.

Be grateful to be you and be grateful for those triggers that get your pain moving in an upward direction. You are transforming you, so watch the show and don't get too upset about anything that may come into your view. It's all just you changing and growing and expanding. You, my dear sweet child of God, are being set free of your denser energies so that you might begin to draw lighter energy to you. This is our goal. Heaven on earth is our goal. Don't fight with energy. Don't struggle to push it back down in you. Don't spew your dense energy out onto your personal reality. Allow the dense energy to move up and out of you as you watch it go. Become the viewer of your life not the judge of your life. Simply "let go and go with the flow."

You are not going to be in a state of healing forever. Once you have released your denser energies you automatically rise up to a whole new level of existence. Many of you have problems and don't create a fear of loss or lack around these problems. Fears around loss and lack are created by the inability to see your life as improving. You may wish for a better life and not receive it due to the fact that you are busy punishing yourself for past injustices, or maybe even something you did or said just yesterday.

The fastest way to get to a better life is to love and accept yourself. As I have stated, if you do not like yourself you will not wish to give yourself gifts. Usually you are giving only to those you care about deeply. Sometimes you do not even feel like giving to them. Watch how you are with your giving. Do you give out of love or do you give out of a need to be loved and accepted? Some of you give but it is not really giving, it is buying another's acceptance and love. Some of you do not give and have found that anger and manipulation work best for you. You use anger and manipulation to keep your family in line and doing your bidding. You see this with cases of extremely obese individuals who cannot get out of bed. They continue to grow in size because their loved ones are afraid to disappoint them and take on their anger by saying, "No, I will not cook that for you," or "No, I will not buy you all that junk food."

Many of you have found that anger and manipulation make you feel powerful and on top of a situation. I will tell you now that anger and manipulation will weaken *you* and bring *you* down eventually. Anger is a very heavy energy and is based in fear and pain. You will find that you perceive those who bow down to these energies to be respectful to you when, in reality, they fear you. Many of you were raised by one, and sometimes more, angry individuals in your life. This does have an effect on you, and on how you live your life and how you perceive the behavior of others. You may not trust others because you fear that they are going to be angry with you at the slightest infraction, or you may have concern that others are too slick and manipulative for you. Either way you will feel intimidated and have a certain amount of fearfulness.

If this fearfulness is constant and ongoing in the

background of your personal beliefs and ideas about people and life, you may find it difficult to trust life and to trust people and, of course, you will not know how to trust yourself. Trust is something that is developed over time, and trust is a fundamental element of life if you are to grow and to thrive.

As you continue to heal by seeing life and yourself differently, you will begin to draw trust into your personal reality. Once you can trust a little, you open the possibility to trust more. It is not so much about trusting others as it is about trusting yourself and your ability to say "no" when you want to. If you had a very angry parent, or guardian, you may "believe" that you are incapable of standing up to anger. Sometimes it's just one angry person, other times it can be a great deal of angry people. As you learn to overcome your fear of anger, you will stop using anger to get your way. It will no longer feel good for you to use your anger to manipulate and control others.

You will find that as you learn to let go of this technique, you may develop a new way to work within your relationships. This new way may include kindness. Kindness is so far north of anger that they could be polar opposites. Kindness has been left out of many of your lives and I wish to see it take a front row seat and become popular once again. Kindness is a form of giving and nurturing. Kindness is a gift in itself. If you were to constantly give out kindness you would lift yourself "up" and you would be lifting your personal reality "up." Give kindness a chance, and whenever possible replace anger with kindness. You do not need to walk around all day with a smile on your face (although that would be nice to see), but it would be helpful to you in your search for health and wealth to begin to give off the energy of kindness.

This will allow you to be kind to yourself also. Most of you require huge amounts of kindness and acceptance at this point in your evolution. You also require forgiveness for anything that you may be judging yourself for. You are not the only one with a difficult upbringing. The people who raised you may have had very angry and manipulative caregivers also. This is a cycle and you can end this cycle of anger and manipulation. You will find that if you are constantly criticizing and finding fault with others, you probably were criticized and found lacking by your parents or other guardians. Criticism leads to harsh judgment and harsh judgment is an energy that draws pain and suffering.

Get off the judgment wagon and get on the love train. The love train is a smooth fast ride. The judgment wagon has some very rough terrain to travel through.

You will find that the kinder you can be to yourself, the more you will grow and thrive. You are about to turn your life around, and when you turn your life around you get to move in a whole new direction. How do I know this? Because I am God and I see all of you, and I am sending positive energy into the material plane in small doses (so as not to disturb you too much) so that you might rise "up" and assist yourself in this Grand Awakening. And just what is this Grand Awakening? It is you, all of you, waking up to the fact that you are part of God; and you are the creator of your own personal reality and view of the world that you see. You create it all and I am assisting you in this process of waking up to who you really are.

You think on that for a while as I need to communicate with Liane in private....

The best way to find out how you feel regarding your own self is to watch and see how you judge your own personal behavior. Most of you do not even realize that you judge yourself day in and day out. This has become a sore point for your soul. Your soul lives in you and your soul knows you inside and out. Your soul guides you whenever possible and often you try to do your own thing and not listen to soul.

As you learn to become aware of your many workings, I wish you to become *aware* of the fact that you are soul and you (the soul) lives within your body. Your soul also lives outside of your body and takes many forms. Your soul could be an energy field that runs through you, and your soul could also be an energy field that surrounds you. Soul energy is very powerful and it comes directly from God. Soul energy is the part of you that has no end and is literally eternal. As you continue to change and to grow, I wish you to remember that you are not only flesh and bone and Homo sapiens you are also energy and eternal.

You will find that the vast majority of you do not think of yourselves as eternal. You think of yourself as a human being, and once in a while you allow yourself to actually *feel* that there may be something more to you. As you continue your growth into awareness, you will actually begin to feel this part of you that is known as soul. Soul is also very powerful and is the creative part of you. You don't so much have a soul as you are a soul. You not so much are a soul as you contain all that soul is. Soul is God energy at work in you. Soul is you at your best. Soul is the part of you that goes on eternally. Soul is often the best of you and you don't even realize that you are part of it. It is as though you have this huge, eternal part of you that you are totally and completely unaware of.

This part of you does not require your attention to do its work. This part of you can survive without you ever becoming aware of it. This part of you often guides you through your day. This part of you has the ability to lift you up when you are down. This part of you has the ability to create for you. This part of you is directly from God and is part of the creative force of your life. This part of you may step forward from time to time to create for you. This is done with your unconscious desires. Soul cannot move in and take over your creations without your permission. You must desire soul to come to the forefront of your life. You do this by becoming *aware* that you have this part of yourself that you hide from yourself.

How many of you get up each day and think, "I'm going to *allow* my soul to guide me today?" And how many of you allow your soul to literally communicate with you? "Impossible to do," you say. Not so impossible! Look at this book you are reading. I wake this woman up from sound sleep and I whisper to her that I would like to write; and before you know it she is up in a dark room, turning on a light so that she might see the lines of her notebook and allow God to move her hand across the page to channel information from within. Where does this information that you are reading come from? It comes from God via the soul. You each have this connection to God and you each may learn to communicate directly with God. It is not such a big deal really. If you live in a field of potentiality and all possibilities, then absolutely anything is possible. If you want it bad enough you will find a way, simply because you are made up of creative force which is soul, or God force within you.

Aren't you magical! Aren't you wonderful! And you don't even know that you are. So, what does this all have to do with wealth? Not a whole lot, but it does have to do with the fact that you don't really know who you are, and how you are put together, and what makes you up. Please stop judging you. You are far greater than you now realize.

The most often felt emotion on earth is fear, which

leads to mistrust. Fear causes you to mistrust and fear pushes away love. Love is the highest vibration, and a state of love will draw all good things into your life. Did you ever notice how when you are feeling great love, the world simply feels like a wonderful place? Did you ever notice how when you are feeling great love, you have no worries? Love is the conquering hero when it comes to energy.

So, I would like you to begin to love! Love you and love all that you are; and this will lead to gratitude of being you, and this will lead to self acceptance, and this will lead to you being considered wonderful by your own self. When you get to the point that you see yourself as wonderful, you will know self-love. Self-love is the number one most important emotional feeling to carry. Self-love allows you to *know* that you are the best "you" that you can be. You are not here to be second best, you are here to be the very best "you" that you can be.

When you can *feel* that you are the best "you" possible, you will feel so good about life that you will no longer fear life. You will face any and all situations from a state of blissful acceptance. You will be capable of allowing life to unfold before you in the most wonderful way. You will have moved into acceptance which allows you to let go of your stranglehold on fear. As stated before, most fear stems from pain and is related to a fear of loss or lack in some area of life, be it emotional loss or material loss. When you have moved into total self-love you will *see* the gifts of your life in a whole new way. Instead of judging each new situation that appears in your life as bad (or uncomfortable) until you can become accustomed to it, you will immediately see each new situation as a potential gift. This will allow you to skip the judgment process, which holds your gifts at a distance, and move right into the receiving aspect of creation.

As you begin to truly love and accept your own self, you will automatically be drawing the highest vibrations into your life. The highest vibrations lift you "up" and add to your life. The highest vibrations allow you to float above the denser vibration of "fear of lack and loss." If you are floating above these denser vibrations you do not feel them. This means that you no longer *feel* loss and lack, and your life begins to reflect back to you that which you are *feeling*. In this case it would be self-love and acceptance. Self-love and acceptance lead you to the higher realms of receiving. Being a magnet in the universe can be difficult when you are drawing the denser energies to you. When you are drawing the lighter energies to you, being a magnet in the universe will always be a wonderful, uplifting thing.

Be uplifted! Uplift you by loving and accepting you. Start where you are and *accept* you just as you are this very moment. Accept you exactly as you are without concern for how you look or how you feel. Know that you can change and grow into the most wonderful, creative being and you can create the most wonderful and magical life for yourself. How freeing to know that it all begins and ends right inside of you. How wonderful to know that you are the cause of your view of your reality, and how wonderful to know that you can change your view at any given moment. Let go of your fear and allow love into your life. Let your fears float away from you and allow trust to become a part of you again.

As you learn to allow trust back into your life, you will find that you are creating a new reality for yourself that is based on the accepted fact that "life is good." This fact will be a reflection of your belief that you are good. This belief will be a direct reflection of your own love of self. So, as you learn to accept you just as you are, I would like you to know that you will be accepting God just as God is. God is you and when you reject any aspect of you, you are rejecting the creative, divine being that you are. Do not reject you. Allow you to be loved and nurtured so that you might grow and evolve into the magnificent being that you are. You are the light of your world and you do not hold yourself in very high esteem at this time.

I will now suggest that you read *The Book of Love* which will assist you in loving you. This book was written in such a way that it will open you up to the idea of self-love. As you read, I would like you to remember that you are the most valuable person in your life because you are creating your life as you go....

---

*A*s you might imagine, it is not so difficult as you think to become wealthy. You first draw money to you, and you then invest or save wisely. The most difficult part for you is to imagine how you will *feel* when you have great, unlimited wealth. You mostly feel undeserving and this will of course change. You also feel unworthy and this too must change.

The quickest and easiest way to feel deserving and worthy is to forgive yourself and allow yourself to feel loved, and worthy, and deserving. You have put yourself down, and now you are going to raise yourself up by allowing yourself to be considered good and wonderful. You need not impress anyone but yourself. Most of you do not wish to be accepted and loved because you feel it would cost you in some way. It will not cost to be accepted and loved by you. You are the one who matters most in your life, and you are the one who is affected most by your thoughts and judgments and revenge and anger.

Here is the biggest problem in being a creative being: "You cannot avoid your own thought energy." Thoughts are energy and this thought energy runs through you and affects you in more ways than you can count. You have no idea how strongly your thoughts affect not only your behavior, but also your physical body. You are shooting arrows into you every time you think vengeful and unkind thoughts. Let this type of creating go. Allow only uplifting, good and kind thoughts to run through you. If you cannot allow yourself to have good thoughts, you will eventually break down your physical body with the power of your negative judgments.

Now, I am not saying that you do wrong or are sinning here. What I am telling you is that there is an effect to negative thinking, and the effect does have an adverse reaction within the physical and emotional body that you live in. We want to get you to a place where you have pleasant thoughts and pleasant emotions. For some of you this may sound boring. You are so accustomed to the stimulation of harsh judgment and debate that you literally thrive on the energy of being right. You feel this "right" energy as one would feel a stimulant. I want you to feel happy, and if your happiness is based on being right, you will have to let go of this pattern if you wish to rise up to a level of receiving that is conducive with wealth and prosperity. Wealth is a receptive form of energy and wealth does not block everyone else in an effort to be happy. Wealth is "open"-ended and allows the flow of energy to and from the receiver. Wealth is only blocked by resistance. Resistance is blocking and pushing away energy. When you judge others as not good enough, you are creating a flow of energy running through your own body and psyche that says, "You are not good enough." If you are not deemed "good enough," you will not receive.

This is how energy works. Energy does not judge and is not ruled by morals. Energy simply flows and changes and moves and grows. Get aboard the flow of energy by letting go of grievances that may be holding you hostage. You are a flowing energy spirit, and you are keeping you grounded by playing in the denser energies. Rise "up" to the lighter energies, and you will see big changes in your life and in your personal reality. You are not meant to be put "down" by judgment and low self-esteem. You are meant to rise "up" to love and acceptance.

You will learn that the best way to let go of judgment is to learn tolerance. Once you learn tolerance you may then take the next step "up" to acceptance. You are not here to put yourself down, and that is exactly what you are doing each and every time that you judge something or someone. You must find your way to the middle and learn to flow with life in order to receive from life.

You will begin to see the gifts that you so desire by allowing yourself to become as loving as possible. Love is a very high vibration and love will allow you to clear fear from your body. "So, why aren't all rich people loving?" – you ask. The majority of wealthy individuals have obtained wealth through work and often through inheritance. Love is a direct result of caring for and nurturing. When you care for and nurture your wealth it will grow. Money is not only matter, it is energy. In the world of energy you will find that it is most important to nurture it so that it might multiply. If you have spent your life begrudging those who have more wealth than you, you may not be in a position to love and nurture wealth.

Each of you has set up your own individual life path based on what you wish to accomplish this particular lifetime. Some of you intentionally came in to earth this lifetime to experience lack and loss, in an effort to learn particular lessons. These lessons vary from individual to individual and could be as simple as wanting to learn empathy for those who suffer great loss.

As you learn empathy you begin to relate to the suffering individuals. As you relate to them you literally can imagine their pain and understand their struggle. Now that you have this affinity with poor struggling individuals, you no longer judge them as stupid or lazy or just incompetent. I assure you that if you judge them as stupid, lazy and incompetent the energy of this thought belief is running through your body and sending signals out into the universe that say, "I am stupid, lazy and incompetent." This will draw to you the gifts that are deserving of someone who is lazy and incompetent. And who decides which gifts such a person should receive? You do! You have it set in your mind just how deserving and how much an individual who is stupid, lazy and incompetent should receive and, of course, since you are a magnet drawing your personal reality from the field of potentiality, you draw to you that which you order. In this case your belief is, "Send them nothing because they do not deserve."

Please watch your thoughts and come over to love. Let go of any preconceived notion that some people do not deserve wealth. What you are doing is ordering your reality from the field of potentiality and the order is, "Do not send money, it is not deserved." You will find that you do not consciously block the flow of money to you, however, you are deeply embedded in some of your beliefs and they are actually supported and enhanced by your society. Your society is filled with those around you who see life a certain way. You literally pressure one another to see life "your way," and your way is simply the way that has been programmed into you and then reinforced to stay in place. Let go of any desire, or habit you may have that puts others down in any way. You are simply putting you down and taking away the possibility of "you" receiving the gifts of this world.

Become generous of mind. Give love and understanding and compassion, and give nurturing to those who you see as less than you. You do not need to go out into your streets and work with the homeless. You may stay at home and change your mind and your beliefs and become a very generous and giving individual. Generosity of thoughts and beliefs goes a very long way. Open up to the *idea* of love and acceptance and you will be opening up the flow of gifts into your life. When you change your thoughts from, "She is so lazy and doesn't deserve to receive that much money" to, "She deserves great wealth," you will be sending an order out into the field of potentiality that says, "I deserve great wealth."

The universe and the field respond to you as though you are the only one here. All messages sent from you are then processed and returned to you. There are other ways of creating, and collective minds working together can bring forth healing and great shifts in energy. For right now, and the purpose of this book, we are discussing "you" and how you create your day to day reality. I will be discussing collective energy signals in a later book, but, for now we will stay within the parameters of your personal reality.

So, as you see others, who you do not necessarily *accept* as good and enlightened beings, I wish you to change your mind and look for the good in them, and if possible the God in them. This is so difficult for most of you as you have based your life on having good judgment. Your *idea* of good judgment is to put others down if you see that they do not measure up. When you tell the field (universe) that they are not good enough, the field will send you "not good enough."

Please be careful how you treat yourself with your thoughts. You may see the world and people as good or, you may see the world and people as bad. You are not really seeing the truth of the matter. You are only "seeing" that which you are projecting out into your personal reality. Change your mind and your reality will change.

☙❧

You will begin to see how you desire to become all that you can be and this will lead to the discovery of you – the spirit. You are multi-layered and you are multi-faceted, and you do not yet realize how you are a spirit who moves and lives within human form.

You are meant to discover your true identity and, in the process, you will discover your traits and your abilities as spirit energy. You are adaptable and you are changeable. You are creative and you are flexible and flowing. So, why do you suppose you do not flow as well as you can? I do believe it is time to tell you about creation and the beginning of time. You have been returning to earth since the beginning of time in an effort to undo what you have done in previous lives. You continue to return out of a desire to get it right. The goal is to *remember* who you really are while in the field of matter. When you are in the material plane you do not recognize your true self. The true self is spirit and the true self allows you to create at will.

You are constantly returning to earth in an effort to remember who and what you truly are, while being enveloped in the material plane. Density requires that you maintain a certain level of density in order to be compatible. Compatibility is necessary when entering matter, so that you do not destroy matter and cause it to implode in on itself or to collapse. You are energy that vibrates at such a high rate that you require a drop in your vibration to be able to enter matter.

So, as you enter the field of matter you become one with it. If you do not become one with it, you do not make it in. So, we have you, the spirit, entering matter and to do so you switch from spirit vibration, which is extremely high, to matter vibration which is extremely low. You now have a high energy being (spirit) entering a low energy field (matter). As you take hold and get a good grip on matter and the technique of vibrating much slower *you begin to lose consciousness* to the fact of your true identity. You forget that you are spirit and part of the spiritual vibration that takes up all space and time. You *narrow* your perception to a tiny pinpoint and you allow the vastness that is you to collapse to a tiny pinpoint of your true vastness.

You are now so tiny that you are unrecognizable as spirit and you are deep within the realms of matter. Some of you (most of you) go completely and utterly unconscious and do not wake up to your true identity until long after the death of your body. What you are looking to achieve here is *consciousness*, awareness that you are spirit and as such you are God. How wonderful to wake up to the fact that you are God come to earth, or the field of matter, and you are aware while *in* matter that you are this divine being. You are energy and the energy that you are comes directly from God. God is creative and God is everlasting and God is omnipotent!

So, what does that make you? You are God, and you are entering matter in an effort to discover your true identity while in this dense field. You might think of it as a game that you play with yourself. Hide and seek is very popular in childhood and you are hiding you from you. The name of the game is "hide God." You spend all your time looking for God; when in actuality, God is right inside of you. You worship God when, in actuality, you are worshiping your own creativeness. You are so special and so magnificent and so incredibly beautiful and you do not see your true beauty.

As you go about your day today I wish you to keep one *thought* in mind. This thought is simply "I am God." Can you do it? Can you own who and what you are?

You will begin to see very subtle changes in your view of how well you are supported by life once you achieve a certain level of appreciative recognition. Right now you may not appreciate all that you currently have in the way of wealth, but as you continue to respect and nurture your wealth you will increase its value and it will grow. Anything that you love in life is affected by your love energy. What you love, you usually draw to you in one way or another. If you love a new model of car you may not immediately draw it to you, however, you will begin to see this model more and more often. You will be focused on it and this puts it in your attention. When you pay attention to something, you may begin to obsess over it and often you want to overcome the desire to obsess over it. Obsession can lead to worry and discord.

If you are constantly worried about money and trying to figure out how to make ends meet, you can get your energy all worked up into obsessive worry and this may lead to further complications for you.

Obsessive worry is one of the most confusing and frustrating of energies. Obsessive worry breaks down your cellular strength and causes stress within the mental and emotional bodies. Once the emotional and mental bodies are stressed, you will begin to feel a breakdown in the physical body. You may even worry yourself into ill health and early death by depression, or heart attack. This is of course an extreme example, but it is stress induced.

The easiest way to let go of worry is to trust! If you can talk yourself into *believing* that everything will work out for the best, you will assist your mental and emotional bodies in achieving a great release of endorphins, and other chemicals that literally assist the cells in your body to stay strong and vibrant. You might say that stress and worry over finances (or anything else) ages you and breaks you down. The lack of stress allows you to function at a much healthier level. And a positive thought process such as, "life always supports me and life is good" allows you to *feel* supported and loved.

This is why I would like you to love yourself and to trust yourself. If you cannot love and trust yourself at this juncture, it would be good if you could love and trust the creative force, which most call God. If you cannot love and trust the creative force, then find something you can love and trust. Trust in a friend, or trust an institution such as a hospital, or trust nature. You will be healthier and happier if you have someone to trust or something to trust. Trust is necessary for the evolution of man, and a lack of trust, or what becomes mistrust, leads to conflict within the body and outside of your bodies in your personal reality. You might say that the more trust you have, the more peace of mind that you will have. The more trust you have, the greater your ability to love and to *accept* love.

If you do not trust, you will not be open to love and you will not be open to other gifts that life, in its wisdom and glory, might be offering you. If you have extreme mistrust, you will not recognize the gift when it arrives. If you do not recognize it, you will more than likely judge it. If you judge it, you will become disillusioned with the *idea* that life is a giver of gifts; and your own personal reality will begin to suffer from a lack of trust that everything is good and you are supported by life. You will fall out of love with life and the magic that life contains. You will see life as humdrum and maybe even a struggle. You will no longer love life, and this loss of love for life will allow you to slip into the lower energies of stress, worry and depression.

You can literally raise yourself back up with a little trust in life. Life is not so bad as some of you have made it out to be. Life is actually quite miraculous once you get the hang of how to *see* the miracles. Once you learn to see the miracles they begin to occur more often. Why? Simply because you will have created an energetic thought pathway to them. Believe in miracles and believe in trust and you will draw the magic of life to you. You are a creative being and you may draw whatever you *allow in* to your life to you. Allow love and trust and be grateful for all that you do have now. This will create great waves of positive energy to begin to flow to you. For some of you, trust will be most difficult. For others, trust has already become second nature for you. Allow trust and you will be allowing for all possibilities to come your way. Without trust you sit alone with your worry and fear. With trust you stand tall and expect the best. Give trust a chance and trust will begin to give you new life!

You will begin to understand how your energy affects the world around you when you begin to calm down, and slow down, and look at what is occurring in your personal reality. Most of you spend your life complaining about your losses and celebrating your gains. When you can learn to accept any loss as part of the equation that leads to a gain, you will be learning to work *with* the flow of energy. The interesting thing is that once you learn to accept loss as part of the equation, you will be accepting reality as it really is.

Waves go up and they go down. Energy moves in waves and often energy builds and then subsides. If you do not allow for the ebb and flow, you are cutting the energy pattern in half and not allowing the creation of this particular event. You may have been drawing something beneficial into your life; and by rejecting the ebb or flow portion of this event, you change what you are creating into something different. You basically change the creation that was sent out from you, into a different form. You may have asked for, or ordered, something specific from the field of potentiality, or the universe; and when you receive it, it does not look anything like what you requested.

If you are really impatient you may change the direction of this energy many times, and all of these changes show up in your life at some point if you do not block them. You might say that you have a vivid imagination, and this vivid imagination is running amuck with no one in charge. This would be okay if it weren't for the power of blame, guilt and judgment. When you add blame, guilt and judgment to the mix, you now have curved the energy into a whole new direction. You are then disappointed that your creation (that you personally ordered) has not arrived, and so you begin to blame or judge God, or life, or yourself; and now we have really *bent* the energy of this creation into something else that is nothing close to your original request, or order, from the universe to you.

So, stay calm and *trust!* Trust God, trust life, trust you and trust the universe. You get so impatient and then you begin to blame life or yourself for not delivering your good to you. Blame diverts everything good and brings *you* guilt. You now have created another block to receiving abundance, as guilt sends out a message that says, "Punish me!" You want to send out a message that says, "*Reward* me!" So, here you sit and you cry for help and you wonder when your life will improve, and it is all up to you. Can you change how you create and begin to allow the energy that you send out to be good, and positive, and rewarding? Think good, positive, rewarding thoughts and these energies will begin to heal you and to change you.

It is not often that I am allowed to speak freely about

how you create pain and problems for yourself. I am most grateful to have this opportunity and Liane has allowed me to go beyond her current level of understanding to deliver this message to you. Allow God/creation/spirit/the creative force into your personal reality and you too will converse with the God force that you literally contain. You will be able to connect to the information of the universe that is available to any and all. You will be allowed to receive insights that are not necessarily common in your current reality. You will find that you contain rivers of information *within* you that you are not currently accessing. It is all there *within* you! You have all that you require to create as a conscious human being right inside of you.

Stop and listen! Really listen to what is going on inside of you. Become *aware* of your inner workings and your true identity. You are connected to God. You do not have a line or string that connects you. You are literally part of the body of energy that is God. You live *in* God and you breathe in God each and every day. God is the love and the light of this world. Come over to love and let go of your fear and judgment. You are safe! You never die and you never end – not ever……

You are often confronted with fear of not having enough and you are also confronted with fear of not being enough. You will find that as you release these two fears, you will begin to relax into "enough." "Enough" will become your new label and you will let go of your hold on "lack." As "enough" becomes your new thought, you will begin to draw to you "enough" energy to supply your needs. If you then are able to stretch your thoughts to the level of believing that you are "more than enough," you will be drawing to you "more than enough."

Thought is a process that is strongly affected by what you see and how you feel. If what you see is "not enough" you will draw more of "not enough." Your seeing "not enough" creates a direct belief response of "not enough." So, you can see why I ask you to look for the gifts so that you might become grateful for all that you now have. In this same way, you will become thankful for being all that you are and loving all that you are. This love of self changes your fear from "not enough" to "very good indeed." This self acceptance will draw to you all that is good, and you will begin to feel that you are "enough." With self-esteem you gain self-love, and with self-love you gain your own wealth and your own support in the field of all possibilities that you exist in. If absolutely anything is possible then you are the chooser and the decision-maker of your life possibilities.

You get to decide who you will be and how you will live your life based on "belief." Your beliefs are powerful and they determine your reality on this plane. Each individual, personal reality is set up by the individual, and is changed only by the individual creator of that particular reality. Many of you spend your time and your energy trying to change others, when it would be most advantageous to spend your time and your energy changing you. Change is easy! You do not believe it is, simply because you feel stuck. You feel stuck in your reality and you feel stuck in life. I want you to set yourself free and begin to flow with life and begin to raise your vibration to one of love. Love is all that is of any importance. Love is the highest vibration available to you on this material plane. We are not speaking of romance here. We *are* speaking of true unconditional loving acceptance.

Come over to love and let go of fear. Fear keeps you stuck. You will know fear when you see it. Fear does not *accept*.

Fear judges and criticizes and blames, and feels guilt and pain. Fear is dense and heavy and slows your vibration to the point of stopping you from lifting "up" to the higher vibrations. Fear is stuck in a low and slow space and love is in a higher, free space. You can "lift" yourself "up" to love by changing you. Do not concern yourself with others. Allow everyone to find their own creative power and abilities. If you wish to spend your time lecturing others on how to live, you are holding you both back. The fastest way to show others how to live at a higher vibration is to let them see how you are living at a higher vibration. This does not take lecturing and pushing at them to be better, or "more like you." "More like you" is not what others require.

What others require is to be more like them. You each play your own role in life and you know on a deep subconscious level what your plan for your life is. Do not become what others want you to be. Become what your spirit and soul are guiding you to be. When others are telling you how to change, I highly suggest you allow them to say what they must, then go on about the business of creating your reality as you choose to. You are the creator of your world, and you live in your life and you experience the causes and effects of *your* energy field. You will know deep within you what feels good for you and what causes you problems.

Many of you have known for years that you have characteristics that draw and create problems for you, but you continue to hold on to these behaviors simply because you believe they serve you. Mostly they become a form of manipulation in dealing with others, and so you continue to hold on to these characteristics, and go into denial as to the effects that they can and do draw into your personal reality. You find them useful in the moment and then you continue to lean on them for support. Criticism is a prime example. If someone says something that pushes your buttons you may zing them back with a sharp criticism. This gets them to back off (in some cases) and allows you to feel a little more powerful in the process.

What you have actually done is to unload some of your own self-criticism onto this individual, so now you feel better because you have unloaded some of this very heavy and dense energy that you carry within you. You are now free of some of your stored up criticism and so you feel relief. This makes you want to hold on to this tool of criticizing in the future. So, if you hold on to criticism as a tool you will draw more conflict or criticism to you, simply because you carry so much of this energy in you.

So, what should you do or how should you respond if someone criticizes you or pushes your buttons? Simply say, "Thank you for sharing your insight with me." This allows you to move away from criticism and manipulation. You are now in a neutral space which *accepts* the flow of the energy, but does not take it on. You are now allowing it to flow right past you, or through you, without blocking it and trapping it *in* you and, by so doing, making it an energy part of you. If you do not feel that you can be so gracious and accepting as to say, "Thank you for sharing your insight" you might say simply, "I see;" meaning you see or understand where this person is coming from. This does not mean that you agree with this individual's criticism of you or even their point of view. It does mean that you see, or understand, that this person might have a perspective that is based on his or her personal experiences that is completely different than yours. You are now allowing this individual to have their perspective while you retain your own. In this way you are not blocking the energy and the possibility of creating greater conflict in your personal reality is lessened.

This is the goal. Less conflict in your life means more peace. More peace means smooth sailing, simply because peace draws more peace to it. Conflict draws conflict, and love and acceptance draws love and acceptance. You see in your life (your mirror reflection) that which you carry *in* you. Carry peace by letting go of conflict and judgment and criticism. Come home to love and joy and happiness. When you are so busy being "right" it is difficult to draw happiness to you. Some of you are so dependent on criticism and conflict that it will be difficult to pull you "up" to the higher vibrations of love and acceptance.

Let the energy flow right on by you. Acceptance is actually a flow of energy that will make you feel very good and very powerful. It takes a very strong person to say, "I accept you just as you are." There is no fear attached to this kind of unconditional love.

※

You will begin to feel changes in how you view your own personal reality once you begin to change your thoughts and your beliefs. You will then begin to shift the energy that is stored within the cells of your body. Cellular memory is something that you are just now beginning to learn about. Each cell in your body carries information, and this information has a big effect on your personal reality as well.

So, what you are made up of and how you have judged past experiences affects you in the present moment. If you carry huge stores of judgment, you will be drawing lots of judgment to you. What you will wish to do, in order to change what you draw, is to reprogram your own cellular memory. One of the best ways to do this is to retrace your steps, so to speak, in order to learn what you have learned, in order to release what you have learned.

Say you were taught early on in life to believe in a

punishing God. Now you are an adult and you may still *believe*, on some level, that God punishes you for your sins. This *belief* affects you on many levels and vibrates at a slower rate than energy of a *belief* like, "God never ever punishes anyone. God is true unconditional love."

Now you contain this judgment call or belief in you that says, "God punishes and each individual will face his maker in the end," and it affects you to the extent that you may carry certain fears regarding this situation should it occur. As you go through life you will begin to expand this fear of a punishing God just by *expanding* you; and how do you expand? Simply by the splitting or division of cells. So now instead of a single cell that carries the slower fear energy of "God judges," we now have two cells carrying this fear. When these two cells split and divide we will then have four cells carrying this slower vibration of fear and drawing four times the fear energy to you. So, as your cells split and divide, the thoughts or memory beliefs in them split and divide and grow. This is how you will ascend. In the same way that your cellular memory splits and divides with the cells, you can reprogram your own cells with new thoughts, beliefs and memories. Remember the good things in life! Let go of the fearful things and hold on to the loving memories. You may need to start at the beginning and see your life in a whole new way.

I realize that many of you have had great abuse in your life, but you can and may change it into a growth situation, and even a positive situation if you are tired of carrying this heavy dense energy, and wish to move on to something lighter. I have channeled a great deal of information through Liane on this exact subject in our *Loving Light Books Series*. This series guides you, the reader, into your own inner realms and workings. If you are interested in changing how you view your own personal reality and how to see it differently you might enjoy this series.

So far you are not doing too badly when it comes to

change. You find change worthwhile when you are told that it can improve your life, and add to your life. The main thing to remember is that you draw to you that which you contain, simply because that which you contain is sending out signals that order your life from the field of all possibilities. Come on over to love energy which is the highest, fastest energy you can send out, and let go of fear which is the densest energy.

Examples of fear energy would be guilt, judgment, criticism, anger, revenge, discontent and aggression. These energies do not come from love they come from fear. Examples of love energy are kindness, generosity, joy, peace, grace under pressure and acceptance. Flowing with the energy comes from love. Blocking the flow comes from fear. Allow life to unfold for you and allow love to heal you. The easiest, fastest way to heal you, and subsequently heal the personal reality that you are projecting, is to love you! Begin now to love you to the core. Love your body, love your personality, love your spirit, love every little and big part of you. Give you so much love that your cells begin to release their fear.

When you fill your cells with positive loving thoughts they will double those positive loving thoughts when they split and divide. You cannot carry fear where there is love. They are opposing energies. Love is the absence of fear, and fear is the absence of love. Think of love as "light." If you turn on a light where does the darkness go? It simply vanishes or disappears. Allow the fear in you to disappear. Allow yourself to expand in love and you will draw to you the gifts of love. You will be gifting yourself from the field of all possibilities on a daily basis.

Now you may be blocking, but you can easily "open" to receive by taking on the task of self-love. This is the most important thing you will do in your lifetime. This is why you are here. You are God expressing through matter and you are true unconditional love. You simply need to remember that you are....

You will begin to see how you have always been in a state of unconsciousness as to how you have created what you see in your life, and this will lead to a desire to wake up! Most of you do not fully realize the level at which you do the creating and this allows you to blame others for your own personal reality.

At this juncture in your life it would be a good idea to go within your own personal habits and patterns, in an attempt to uncover your negative feelings regarding life. You have developed habits and traits that allow you to get through life in a way that allows you to be unafraid. You often use your habits as a way of uncovering the worst in individuals and even as a way of uncovering the worst in yourself. You feel that you can operate from a level of mistrust and this will allow you to point a finger at, and blame others, for making your life miserable.

You tend to find it necessary to find someone else to blame when you are unhappy, or miserable, in a specific situation. If you can learn to accept that you have created and drawn each situation into your life for a purpose, you will then be allowed to see the value of each individual situation.

You do not like to see the good in all things, and you rarely see the good in most things. Now is a time to look for the good in all situations. You are learning to rise up to a whole new level of vibration, and this is more easily accomplished if you can come out of harsh judgments and move into acceptance. The energy difference between judgment and acceptance is huge! I know that many of you are afraid to accept certain situations in your life, simply because you do not want more of the same situation. If you can step aside and allow each individual situation to be seen by you as having some value to you, you will be accepting this situation and allowing it to go right on by you.

You only stop the situations that you wish to hold on to. A situation, or an event, that has unfolded before you has done so for a reason. You will be sticking yourself to the situation if you fight it. You must let it go by if you do not wish to get involved and stuck to the event. Say you have a discussion with your parent and this parent decides that you are wrong about your view, or perspective, regarding the topic you are discussing. If you continue to push your point of view at your parent, you are engaging in combat. You are pushing energy at someone who does not wish to receive this energy. Of course, we are assuming in this particular situation that your parent does not wish to change their point of view; and so you push at this parent to change how they see this situation, and eventually you end up with an argument and possibly hurt feelings. Your energy is now fully engaged in this conflict over who is right. This may last for days, or weeks, or months. This could cause a split in the family if other members get involved and take sides.

This is a matter of energy being stopped and pushed at. Had you simply allowed the energy to move past you without engaging it, or blocking it, you would not find yourself in conflict. The need to be right and to blame others is big on planet earth. How can you possibly *feel* self-love when you are constantly engaged in this type of energy conflict?

So, how do we handle energy when it is others who are pushing at us (with their energy) to change? We may step aside and allow the energy to flow right on by. You may begin to allow everything to be what it is and to move by you. You need not block everything and you need not take responsibility for fixing everything. Let it go! Go with the flow of energy! I am not asking you to take the blame that is being pushed at you. I am suggesting that you not engage in conflict by fighting and arguing over who is right and who is wrong.

This will begin to clear some of the more restricted lines of energy (or pathways) that run to and from you. These pathways are important for you if you wish to receive your highest form of good from the universe, or the field of all possibilities. Keep your lines open and free-flowing. Allow yourself to become untangled from the energy you have taken on in the past, by allowing your pathways to relax and calm down, and trust that all is going well and good in your life. Your pathways to you tense when you tense. Your pathways to you open when you open.

When you are in conflict, your pathways are tense and blocked and shut down and unable to receive. Open up and allow energy to flow without shutting off and shutting down. You will be happier and you will move through life with grace and with ease. Trust life and trust you to be the best "you" that you can be. Trust that life is moving you in a good direction and trust that you are loved and protected. If you do not trust you personally, then learn to trust the part of you that is spirit or soul. Some call this the "higher self" or the "God in you." Either way you will be trusting something inside of you that is of a higher vibration. The more you trust this higher vibration in you, the higher it will take you. It *is* possible to totally turn your life over to this part of you, and to simply become the observer of your life. You simply sit back and allow the "God in you" to drive. Take a rest and give up the reins of your life to God. It's not really that scary; and for those who are comfortable with surrender it will feel very, very good.

So, allow energy to move by you and only stop what you want to incorporate into your personal reality. If you do not wish to see conflict in your personal reality, I highly suggest that you flow with the energy and allow peace into your personal space.

You will begin to see great changes in how you create your reality once you begin to recognize how you create your reality.

Suppose you are the eldest child in your family and you are expected to help raise your siblings. As you assist your parents in the task of the upbringing of little ones, you become a responsible little person. You are now taking on an adult role and adult responsibilities, and yet you are just a child. As you continue to assist your parents in this task, you begin to feel more and more *responsible* for the behavior of your younger siblings. This may cause you to begin to resent your brothers and sisters, or it may cause you to become pushy and controlling with them in an effort to get them to follow your guidance.

Now here you are, as an adult, and you still believe that you are in charge and that you know best. Some of you are even called "born leaders" by society. What actually occurred is that you became a very young adult before your time. You are not so much a pushy controller now, as you are a programmed controller. Years of being told to lead and years of being handed extra responsibility have programmed you to become a leader of sorts, or the one in charge. Now you are in a position of being in charge and you find it difficult to simply "let go and go with the flow" of energy.

This is a time to flow and to allow yourself to change. I do suggest that you begin to allow yourself to play and relax a little more, and this will allow you to come out of your feelings of responsibility. Yes! Responsible people are good and even needed in life; however, responsibility is a double edged sword.

You can become so overly responsible that you blame yourself and you blame others when things don't work out the way you think they should. Blame carries a large charge of energy, and blame usually creates guilt as an effect. So now, because blame was sent out that said, "I am guilty, I made a mistake," or, "You are guilty, you made a mistake," we have drawn "guilty" to us. Blame says, "You are guilty" and the field of possibilities responds with, "Okay here's that guilt you ordered."

You now walk around feeling your own guilt, or feeling that others are the guilty ones. However, since the energy is running around *in* you, you are the one who is now riddled with subconscious guilt, and you do not *realize* that you are. You are burdening yourself with this energy that you send out and *receive* back. Let it go! Stop judging you and stop judging them. You have been programmed to be a certain way and now we are changing your programming. Every time you read information that opens your mind to new possibilities, you are allowing yourself to be reprogrammed to *see it all differently*.

I would like you to begin to recognize how you create your reality, so that you might learn to send out love and acceptance and gratitude. Nothing will lift you higher and speed up your energy vibration faster than these three energies. The energy of love is probably the single most powerful energy that you contain. You rely heavily on responsibility and blame in your world. I want you to switch over to love. Just love everyone and everything. I don't care what they have done. If you can see them through the eyes of love and kindness you will lift yourself up to a level of awareness that will allow you to "open up" in a very big way.

Stay open! Do not shut down. Do not draw back into fear and judgment. Allow love to guide you and allow yourself to feel safe in the world by letting go of your labels of good and bad. Everything is energy! There is no good or bad, you simply define life in these terms. As you go along I would like you to keep in mind that absolutely everything is energy. Everything is made up of the *same* energy, as everything has come from the same place.

As you become proficient at "opening up" and allowing yourself to be reprogrammed, you will let go of the blame/guilt game that you play. This will allow you to let go of the good guy/bad guy game that you play. Once you have let go of this programming you will take on new programming which sends out energy from you that says, "We are all innocent, we are all learning to love." Once you are sending out innocence and love, you will begin to receive gifts from the field of all possibilities that say, "Okay, you are innocent and you are loved. Here are your rewards."

You create it all! You send out signals and these energy signals that you send out draw back to you, from the field of all possibilities, that which you have requested. The field does not pick and choose. The field complies with your request simply because you are a magnet that draws certain and specific energies to you based on what is *in* you. So, what is in you? Do you know? Can something as simple as being in charge of your siblings, at a young age, create a pattern in you that you may wish to reprogram? Go *within* and learn what energy is driving your life forward. It's good to know who you are and what is inside of you....

As you continue to develop and to recognize how you create and draw your creations to you, you will become more and more comfortable with this process. You are just now learning how you are the creator of your own personal reality, and the better you become at "gifting" yourself the better your view of life becomes. You see, you control your view of life and you control how you live "in" your world. You are the one who determines whether or not you accept, or reject, every aspect of your created reality. If you continually allow every aspect to be seen as a possible "gift," you will be allowing you to receive a much greater flow of energy into your life. If, on the other hand, you choose not to allow every possibility to be a gift, you begin to close down the flow by judging said possibility as not good enough.

Throughout this entire book I have repeated many times, in many ways, how you create your personal reality and how you view and often judge your personal reality. This is no accident! Repetition is required to get through to your subconscious mind and repetition is required to change your programming. You have literally been programmed by repetition in the past, and this past programming has been most advantageous in certain cases and most destructive in others.

So, as you read you will begin to become *aware* of your own personal programming, and hopefully this will allow you to *shift* upward to a much higher level of awareness. You are reprogramming yourself by searching for, and reading, and learning new ways of seeing yourself and your life. This shift "up" affects the world that you live in and those who live in it with you. Energy is dispersed throughout time and space; and since you are living in a time and space reality, energy will affect all of you. You send out energy and you *receive* energy. It is possible to take on the energy of another simply by living in close proximity with them.

You will find that your close relationships have an effect on you and you have an effect on them. Mostly you try to control one another, however, you also help one another and you disable one another. Some of you actually enable dysfunctional behavior in your closer relationships, and others are put in the position of becoming victims of a close dysfunctional relationship. These more dysfunctional relationships will end when you begin to love yourself enough to end these relationships, and to possibly walk away and move "up" to a more positive way of relating to one another.

Most of you are seeing life and the world as a place of mayhem, and you do not see the world as moving in a good and positive direction. To those of you who *choose to see* the world in this way I would ask you to reconsider. I have channeled a great deal of information (regarding the changes that are taking place) in my other books, so I will not go into detail here regarding this subject. I will, however, ask you to please stop yourself from any negative critique and begin to look for, and draw to you, a more positive view of reality. You see, your thoughts do affect you, and sometimes you push those thoughts and personal views strongly onto others. You look for the weak and try to convert them to your way of seeing reality. In actuality your way is just that! It is simply one way out of billions and zillions of possibilities; and you have settled on this one way of seeing reality because it suits the role that you are currently casting yourself in.

You may see yourself as a victim of life or you may see yourself as a conqueror of life. You will view reality from where you stand and from how you view yourself. Do not push your ideas and thoughts and beliefs onto another until you are vibrating at a much higher rate of awareness please. I do not wish you to project your pain and your fear out onto the rest of the world. Why would you wish to spread negativity and fear? I would most appreciate it if you spread love and joy, and have a good positive attitude towards life and towards the world.

The world is doing just fine! Everything is in divine order. Life will continue to thrive here on planet earth. Please do not pollute her with your fear energy. Send out only pure thoughts and pure love and we will all thrive here. You are literally "requesting" the worst from the field of possibilities when you believe in the worst outcome for planet earth. Don't you see what you are doing? Don't you know how powerful you are? Can't you see through this game that you play? Begin to allow you to be a creator of love and allow everything else to simply fall away.

You will become all that you can be by allowing yourself to see how you create and draw your life experiences to you. If you wish to be wealthy and financially independent I highly suggest you begin to repeat daily, "I am wealthy and independently financially secure." This allows you to begin to convince yourself to *receive* financial independence. If you wish to be healthy I highly suggest you say, "I am healthy and I wish to continue to be healthy." You may wish to put the two together for a very powerful affirmation such as, "I am healthy and wealthy and I wish to continue with this good fortune."

My pen often repeats them together in this way, "The world loves and supports me. I draw wealth and perfect health into my life." Another of her favorites to repeat often is, "Great wealth and perfect health are always flowing into my life." The more you repeat an affirmation the greater the opportunity to receive what you are sending out. At some point the act of sending out gratitude for your positive statements will begin to pay off. An even faster way to draw your desired outcome into your life is to remove your subconscious blocks to receiving. These blocks can be uprooted and sent up and out of you simply by changing the belief patterns that you carry.

Once you begin to change the belief patterns that you carry, you will begin to literally rewire the neurons in your brain. The neurons connect and reconnect depending on strong beliefs backed by strong feelings. Once you begin to change your beliefs to the extent that you are "feeling" new beliefs strongly, you will be rewiring you. This is how you literally change what you draw to you in life. It's all "in" you and it always has been. Man is slow to discover his own inner workings simply because man has been evolving into a better version of himself. Evolution takes time and a little patience. You do not simply change overnight unless you encounter a dramatic experience that affects you profoundly.

I will guarantee you that you will begin to change, and evolve faster, if you let go of the old belief patterns that hold you back and accept a new more expansive view of life. You will not see changes overnight; however, you will see big changes, in a steady flow, that will allow you to *know* on a deep level that you are indeed changing, and as a direct result you see your life experiences differently. Once you see your life differently, you begin to draw new experiences into your life to show you how you are on a better path and life is changing as you change. You do not become a newer version of yourself overnight, however, you do begin to like and even love this new you.

As you begin to like and to love this new you, you will begin to accept *you* more and more. As you *accept* you, you will be accepting life. To accept life is to see life as a gift. To see life as a gift is to see yourself as a gift. You *are* your life! You *are* the creator of all that occurs in your life; and what occurs, or is drawn to you, is a direct result of what you carry *within* you. So to say, "My life sucks" is to say, "I suck!" Allow yourself to change and to grow without putting a great deal of pressure on you to accomplish this transition overnight.

Be patient with you! Be patient with life! You are not going to get where you wish to be by judging yourself as a failure. You are changing and expanding, and growing energetically every time you take in new enlightened information and use it to your advantage. You simply do not *see* the change, as it is done on an energy level. Allow yourself the time it takes to reprogram yourself, and your neurons will begin to reconnect in new positive loving ways. This is important simply because the neurons send signals to the cells in your body, and these signals are received and responded to. Allow your brain to assist you by allowing it the time it requires to reprogram.

You are a sentient being and you are not aware of most of what goes on *within* you. Allow yourself "time" – time to heal, time to reprogram and time to transform into the powerful being that you truly are. You play a game with yourself in order to enter the dense world of matter. You become dense in order to be compatible with the material world. Were you to enter matter as your highest vibration, you would destroy the matter you were attempting to enter. You must lower your vibration in order to enter matter without causing a disturbance. You must dummy down and go unconscious of the fact that you are spirit and actually vibrate at the highest levels. You are only partially *in* matter, and the part of you that remains outside of the material world is fully conscious and fully *aware* of you and your struggle to accomplish your task.

And what is your task? Your task is to enter matter, and by entering it, transform it. You are literally bringing dense energy up to speed by moving it from *within* it. Matter is dense and does not move well. It is not as flexible as it could be. You (spirit you) are transforming matter in an effort to change dense matter into a much lighter version of itself. Why? Because dense matter can be transformed into beautiful shapes and forms. Dense matter can be taught to fly and to flow with energy. Dense matter is stuck and in order to move to the light, which is an extremely high vibration, dense matter must begin to move and to transform to a much higher vibration.

And why is this important? Simply because absolutely everything goes home to the light! Nothing is left out – not even you – no matter how dense you may believe that you are.

※

This is a great time of awakening and it is a time of learning just how powerful you are. It is also a time of learning to love. Man has lost his true nature in his attempt to enter the realms of matter. Man's true nature is spirit. Man is a spiritual being residing within matter. Matter is not the enemy. Matter is simply the form man has taken on. He/she is in costume. He/she does not yet realize that he/she might simply remove the costume and return to the light spirit that he/she truly is.

So, as you go about your day, I wish you to remember that you are a creative energy force who is constantly sending out signals. Those signals draw your life and the events of your life to you. You are a spirit who inhabits a human body, and this spirit who is you is in a position to assist you, and to raise your vibration so that you might fly higher than ever before. This spirit that inhabits you is creative by nature and will assist you in drawing all that you desire into your life. This spirit that is *in* you is God. You carry God right inside of you, and God is actually love and light. Release the love and light that is already *in* you and you will lift yourself to a whole new vibration, which will in turn send out a whole new level of vibrational energy.

This energy that you will then be sending out from you will literally draw miracles and magic into your life. Allow yourself to reach for the stars. Allow yourself to see the light and the love that exists right there within you. When you allow yourself to see the light and the love within you, you will begin to see the light and the love in all of life. It all begins and ends with you. You are now in a position to wake up and begin to see all of life differently. You are in a position that will *allow* you to come "up" out of the denser energies of fear and mistrust and criticism. Please move "up!" Please change! Please see the benefit in being positive and kindhearted and very loving. This is not about helping others and saving them with your love and kindness. This *is* about loving you and saving you with your kindness. Whatever you think – runs through your body. Send love and kindness through your cells. They have been bombarded with judgment and criticism for far too long. When the cells in your body split, the energy doubles and you are left with twice the criticism and judgment that you once carried.

This goes on and on until you are literally consumed with criticism and judgment. Give love a chance to come into *you*. Give love a chance to affect you and to run through the cells of *your* body. Do not let criticism and judgment take over *you*. Allow love and kindness to rule and to reign. Allow love to bombard the cells of your body. Allow love and kindness to rule your life. Allow yourself to give to yourself in the most wonderful way. Allow your love to bombard your cells until they divide and create twice the love *in* you. You will become a walking, talking, love-bomb exploding with the highest vibration possible. Right now you are exploding with anger and rage. Come over to love and kindness. You will *feel* so much better and your health will improve exponentially.

Please give love a chance. Love is your true identity and you have been pushing love aside in favor of the denser energy of criticism. Love gives you gifts and criticism takes away your gifts. Celebrate you by giving yourself the gift of love. With love you will *receive* in a very big way and your life will improve exponentially also.

So, do not hold on to the idea that you must be a tough guy to prosper financially. Financial abundance is a gift and will arrive when you *decide* that you are good enough and lovable enough to *receive*. You may wish to turn on your love and kindness for your own self first. This will allow you to begin to see others with love and with kindness.

You are each walking your own individual path; however, all paths lead to the same end. That end is God; the light; the unconditional love that *is*. You will find yourself on the path to love/light/God and you will most enjoy the transition from heavy energy to lighter energy. Remember, you are an energy producing machine. You may produce light energy or dense energy, and that is what you will draw to you from the field of all possibilities. You can only draw to you that which you contain. What do you contain? What thoughts and beliefs have you been feeding the cells in your body? Good nutrition brings good health on many levels. Allow for good cellular intake by feeding your body only the highest, lightest energy.

It is all so simple. Energy in; equals energy out. Love in; equals love signals going out from you. Criticism in; equals criticism and judgment going out from you. When you are sending a signal that says, "You have been found guilty," you do not *receive* the highest form of gifts from the field. Allow your signals to be the highest vibration possible. Send out signals that draw loving rewards into your life.

Judgment and punishment draw judgment and punishment. Love and kindness draw more love and kindness. Do not blame God for the state of your life. God is pure unconditional love and God is only *allowed* into your life at your request. God does not push aside your wishes, beliefs and thoughts to enter your life. God only enters when *you* invite God in. Invite the creative power of unconditional love into you, by allowing your spirit to come to the forefront of your life and connect with you. This is how you transition into your true nature which is love. Ask God/spirit to become a part of you by asking God/spirit to be you. You already are a spiritual being; you simply have forgotten that you are. By asking spirit to enter your life, you will be assisting yourself in bringing this *awareness* to the surface.

You have so much *in* you that is hidden from you. For now, I would like you to focus on love and kindness. Love and kindness will allow you to calm down and begin to *feel* love and kindness towards your own self. You are so programmed for, and full of, criticism and judgment that you are in a state of low self-esteem. We will raise you "up" to self-worth by running the energy of love and kindness through your cells. Then we will be ready to *receive* the gifts that you so surely deserve. You always get what you ask for. Ask for love and kindness and your gifts will begin to flow!

※

You will begin to see how you are indeed the creator of your personal reality by looking at how you respond to events in your life. If you respond with trust that all is going well, you will always *feel* like life is a smooth ride. This process of feelings affects you greatly, as emotions send strong energy patterns.

When a difficult situation arises in your life it is easily worked through if you are in a state of trust. Without trust you pretty much fall apart and lose your sense of humor altogether. With trust you carry on and move through situations with ease and with grace. Trust is greatly needed at this time, as you are causing huge energy shifts through your lack of trust and your fear, which causes you to struggle with life. Some of you are literally kicking and screaming as you *feel* that you are being dragged through your life. There is a much better way to go through life than to be pulled, or pushed, kicking and screaming through it.

With trust, you literally let down some of your defenses and life is allowed to work through you. You are part of life and nature, and you are affected by life and by nature. You are part of all that you see in the universe and you are part of a much larger picture that you do not see. You are like a fish in a pond and you do not yet *realize* how large the world outside your little tiny pond is. To you this pond that you live in is huge and it is all encompassing. You are so accustomed to being a fish that you do not realize how many other species may exist outside of your little pond. You are a fish living in water and you cannot *imagine* that others would exist outside of your little pond.

You believe that you are the king within your little pond and you try to control everything that occurs within your waters. You are not all there is! There is life that is in existence that you are actually connected to and affected by, and you do not see or concern yourself with anything beyond your pond. When the water in your pond begins to dry up, you begin to blame someone or something. You have totally forgotten your connection to nature, and so you believe that nature is your enemy. Some of you even believe that acts of nature are some sort of punishment from a vengeful God.

Nature is energy. Nature is cause and effect. You affect nature and nature affects you. You are part of nature, and when you get all worked up and angry and afraid, you create a disturbance in the calm water of your tiny pond. When millions of you get excited and worked up and angry and fear-filled, you literally begin to tweak your nervous system and cause energy shifts that in turn cause ripples in the pond that you live in. You are affecting nature simply by the fact that you live *in* nature and you are part of nature. When millions of you create energy ripples in the field in which you exist, you are creating the beginning of a wave. Energy often moves in waves, and waves that are very big create very big changes in the pattern of nature.

You are nature and nature *is* you. You affect nature (or the water that you live in) and nature affects you. Cause and effect! Absolutely everything is cause and effect. It is time to calm down and begin to trust life and trust nature. The more you stir things up with your anger and criticism, the rougher the water becomes. Stay calm. Breathe in and breathe out, and allow yourself to go with the flow. There is no *need* to not trust life. There is no *benefit* in mistrust and criticism. Let it all go. Allow yourself to live in calm waters by allowing yourself to calm down and breathe peace.

Know that you are loved and know that you are safe, and know that you are totally and completely taken care of. You have all that you require to take real good care of you. It all exists right inside of you. Even your answers lie right inside of you. You contain vast stores of information within the cells of your body. You are part of the field of all possibilities and all possibilities are *within* you.

Treat you with a great deal of respect. Love you and be very, very grateful to be you. You are much greater, and larger, and more powerful than you can even imagine at this point in your evolution. You are God!

⁕

*A*s you can see, it is most difficult to get you to a level of awareness that will give you a really good view of reality. For now, we will work on getting you to calm down your current reality enough that you will be allowed to work *with* your current creations. Once you are working *with* the flow of energy that is coming to you, you will then be in a position to change the flow of your current creations.

This is a process of going with the flow in order to

merge with the flow, in order to allow yourself to lead the flow in a whole new direction. Do not worry. You do not get so caught up in the current flow that you do not enjoy the ride. The current flow will take you to a place that is conducive to your lifestyle up until now. You then take the flow in a whole new direction by sending out new positive thoughts, beliefs and ideas. You let go of worry and stress and strife, as these energies will bring you what you do not want. Worry is a message sent out requesting that which you are *afraid* you might receive. If your worry is backed by strong emotional fear it will come into your life faster than if it is not strongly backed by emotional fear.

So, send out "that which you wish to receive back into your life," and accept "that which is occurring" without giving it the power of your critical thinking and critical judgments. This is the basis for creating what you want in your life. Stay calm and always be grateful for the creative power that you are. Know that you create energy shifts in your life, and sometimes you do not *recognize* things that are gifts to you when they arrive. Awareness will give you a lift up in all of your creating. The more aware and on cue you can be when your good arrives, the more impact your good will have on you and in your life.

So, know you and know what you contain that may be affecting you adversely. Do not be afraid of any habit or pattern that you carry within you, as habits and patterns are easily changed. Allow yourself to be all that you can be by allowing everyone and everything to "be." You are part of this vast consciousness that currently fluctuates between unconscious and conscious. As more of you wake up you will bring in greater awareness, and consciousness will continue to expand. You are on a grand journey and part of your fear is based in your unconscious state. You fear what you do not know and, at this stage of your evolution, you literally fear parts of your own self.

Love you and accept you just as you are and you will begin to change your fear of self into love and gratitude of self. This is the fastest way to get to a higher level of awareness and to bring in greater consciousness. Awareness leads to consciousness and consciousness leads to opening up to all possibilities.

We began this book trying to learn about money and how to create great wealth. If you follow the suggestions in this book you will not only draw to you wealth, you will draw to you health and happiness. A happy person is a grateful person. The more gratitude you have in your life the happier you will become; and what does gratitude come from? It comes from not only allowing life to flow, but also saying "Thank you for this." Gratitude is a way of "receiving." Be receptive energy. Stop blocking and begin to "receive."

You are one of the most magnificent creations and yet you are almost completely unaware of your ability to be magnificent. You are beautiful and yet you only value artistic beauty and facial beauty. You do not see beyond the surface to the beauty of your energy. You are one of the most complex creatures and yet you only view yourself as a simpleton of sorts.

You are so vast that you are connected to absolutely everything and everyone, and yet you feel like you are alone and separate. The truth is that you are all one giant being. You see yourself as separate, but what you are seeing are different cells that live and thrive in the same vast body known as "life." Life is "in" you and life is part of everything. You are life, and even in death you are life. You never really die and you continue on and on and on. You are so vast and so spread out that you may never become *aware* of all that you are. All that you are is being made up and expanded as you go and grow. You are constantly becoming more of what you already are. Your energy is going out into the field and creating more. Your body is alive with energy that is constantly creating more. You are a pulsating, thriving life form, and your only problem is your inability to recognize your true greatness.

If you were to see you as you truly are you would be in awe of your greatness. You would never again judge yourself or another. You would *realize* that what you think affects not only you but the entire world. You would know that you are not only 'not' alone; you have never ever been alone. You are in infancy in your state of awakening. You are like a baby who is just now discovering that it has fingers to grasp and hold things. It is just now learning that it has toes and feet and legs that will one day stand and then walk and soon after, run. You do not know who you are and so you are unaware of your abilities. For now, I wish you to concentrate on the energies that will most assist you when you learn to take your first step. "Balance" is important. Once you can balance, you can stand. So, I ask you to stay calm and to think positive thoughts. Trust will keep you level and balanced. Love will move you forward with grace; and gratitude will keep you in a state of grace. Be graceful and gracious in all that you do and you will transform yourself into a most happy and joyful version of yourself.

You are the love and the light of this world and you are just now getting your legs under you to learn to walk. What you don't yet realize, and what no one has told you, is that it is possible for you to fly. You will open to many new ideas in your future and you will begin to *see* your connection to everything that exists. If it's energy, then you are connected to it. If it exists, then you are connected to it. You are part of everything and you have an effect on everything. You are affecting your neighbors and your pets and your plants with your energy. You affect the food that you eat and the air that you breathe.

You are a pulsating living organism and you have abilities that are not only unknown to you, but also unheard of by many of you. Have you heard of telekinesis? Telekinesis is the ability to move objects with your mind, and yes, you can move objects with your willpower and focus of attention. "So, why doesn't everyone do this?" – you ask. Simply because everyone is skeptical and judgmental and will not *accept* this reality. You can only create or experience that which you accept. If you do not accept it as a possibility you will not receive it as a gift. Acceptance is key when it comes to opening the mind. The more potential you can accept, the greater your chance of seeing it as a reality in your world.

So, why don't most of you believe in the possibility of the mind interacting with and moving objects at will? Because you are just too smart! You believe you are smart to judge and to weigh the outcome of possible events, and you do not wish to be made to look foolish. So, bottom line, your fear of looking foolish and sounding foolish stops you from accepting this wonderful ability that you all possess and very few of you use. You will find that this is about to change. You are coming to a point in your evolution that will be most wondrous, as you will discover not only your ability to crawl and walk and run, you will begin to fly! You will begin to soar with knowledge and intuitive wisdom that will allow you to cross dimensions and see realities as never before. You are on your way to becoming all that you can be. You are the creative being that you have always been; only now you will *realize* that it is all you and that you are part of all that is. This is a time of waking up and *realizing* that you can have it all, by simply allowing yourself to have it all.

The best way to create love in your life is to begin to love yourself. Love that is freely moving in you will then begin to affect your life and your personal reality. As you continue to love you, you will begin to draw great love and appreciation into your life. This is a gift! Love and appreciation are two very powerful gifts and they will lead you in the direction of positive flow and balance.

Do not be afraid to love yourself. It is not arrogant and it is not prideful. Love of self is mandatory in your search for perfect health. Love of self will allow the cells in your body to vibrate at a very high speed and this will allow you to heal your body. A healthy body will allow you the freedom to enjoy movement and ease in your daily routine. A healthy body is a very big gift and is a part of being wealthy. Health is considered wealth, and when you are unhealthy you spend a great deal of your wealth to become healthy again. You spend a great deal on health insurance and health recovery and medications; and this could easily be turned around if you would simply send enough love energy through your body. If you were to love yourself totally and completely, you would not age and you would not get sick. With total and complete love running through your body day and night, you would begin to heal all pain and suffering and deficiencies within the body.

Love is a most powerful gift and love is a gift that continues to give. Allow love to be a big part of your life and you will be rewarded in unbelievable ways. Allow yourself to know beautiful, unconditional love-of-self by allowing yourself to accept you unconditionally – just as you are – right now this minute, with no judgments and no criticism. Allow your body to thrive! After all, your body is how you process your creative energy. Your body is your magnet that is drawing to you from the field of all possibilities. Your body carries the energy of your thoughts and beliefs and ideas. Don't you think of yourself as the most valuable asset you own? Aren't you a priceless instrument that must be loved and nurtured and valued and respected?

You are the most valuable possession that you own. *You are actually the only possession that you truly own and you are priceless.* So, how do you treat this valuable possession that you own? Do you take real good care and maintenance of it, and do you keep it safe from damaging thoughts and judgments and criticism? How good are you to you? How much do you prize you? How conditionally do you love your body? Do you love you only when you look good in your mirror? Do you love you only when you have no wrinkles on your skin? Do you dislike or reject parts of you? Is your hair good enough for you? Is your butt small enough or big enough? Are your eyes the right color to suit you? Do you *believe* and *accept* the idea that you must look a certain way and behave a certain way? Are you concerned that others judge your appearance and so you feel ashamed of how you look?

All of this is conditional! You cannot truly accept and love you until you accept and love *all* of you. Please begin to see past your judgments and criticism. You will be so much happier and healthier, and you will begin to appreciate the valuable asset that being "you" is. You are a gift! *You* are the most powerful being and you do not even recognize that you are. You are so totally unconscious that you do not see how you are destroying your greatest asset which is self-love. Self-love will create the most unbelievably beautiful life for you. Your personal reality will thrive when fed a steady flow of love energy. Please love you!

You will become very adept at the practice of creating by *allowing* life to unfold before you. As a spiritual being you found it quite easy to flow with energy. As a spirit you are literally shown how energy moves and how to flow with that movement. As a human you begin to control the movement in an effort to develop your creative abilities. What you do not realize is that you are changing the energy simply by judging it and criticizing it. You have a direct effect upon energy, and you can affect energy in a positive way by seeing it as good.

Once you learn to see how your thoughts and beliefs have a direct effect on energy, you will allow for more freedom of expression and less judgment. The reason you do not trust energy to respond correctly, or in ways that you like, is that you are not a trusting being. You have lost your ability to trust and you have lost your ability to flow. You must regain this ability in order to *see* what is really going on here. Right now you only see from a negative perspective that has been filtered through your fear and mistrust. Once you get the feeling of trust back into your life, you will find your balance and it will be easy for you to flow. When it becomes easy for you to flow, you will begin to have greater trust and you will enjoy the role that energy plays in your life.

If you do not enjoy the role that energy plays, you may find yourself trying to extinguish energy in various ways. The more you try to extinguish energy, the more difficult it will become for you to live happily. You see, you *are* energy and if you do not trust energy you have a very big problem, don't you? You are not trusting you and you are not trusting life to provide life-sustaining energy to you. If you do not trust life and you do not trust energy, what do you trust? Right now you trust judgment and you trust fear. Many of you trust fear to the extent that you actually believe it to be healthy to fear. It is not healthy to fear and you do not gain anything by using fear as a tool. As you learn how energy works, you will see that fear actually destroys and bends and misshapes energy. Fear distorts energy and causes energy to move in ways that are destructive to the flow.

As you continue to learn to trust life and to trust energy, you will actually be trusting you. You are the one who is learning to flow with life and, as you trust, you run trust through the cells in your body. This will allow your body to *feel* trusted and this will allow you to *feel* trusted. How would you feel if no one ever trusted you? This is what you do to *you*, day in and day out, by constantly running the energy of mistrust through your body. Do you wonder why so many take medication to calm down? Do you wonder why so many do recreational drugs to the point of addiction? Do you wonder why so many stuff themselves to the point of obesity in an effort to not feel? It is not a good way to live and it is not a good way to treat your body, mind and psyche. Fear has ruled for so long that you actually know fear better than you know love. Fear is your constant companion, and fear is multiplying each time a cell *in* you divides.

Please see the benefit in coming over to trust. Please allow yourself to *know* that everything is really in a good way and everything is going to be okay. You will sleep better when you see better. Right now your vision is so distorted that you see only fear and lack and loss. You can change your perspective as easily as you change channels on your television. See love, see beauty, know trust and *accept* the flow of your life. You will *receive* all that you require when you trust the flow. You will move into a state of grace once you let go of fear and mistrust. Can you do it? Can you let go of fear and mistrust and come over to love and trust? Love and trust will create greater gratitude for all the gifts that arrive from being in a state of love and trust. You will *feel* so much better when you are trusting *you*.

You have been holding yourself down with your mistrust of self. Now it is time to lift your self up, and to receive in a very big way!

※

You will begin to create wealth and health when you are moved to the higher vibrations. The higher vibrations allow you to receive and to move freely in life. Think of the higher vibrations as a way to move with ease through your life. Many of you hold tight to your ways and control life at every turn. You are so afraid of loss that you actually think it might be dangerous to encourage anyone to "go with the flow" and "trust that life will deliver your good to you."

You are so afraid of lack and loss that you think you must work hard and try even harder. You encourage this in your young, and yes, this is one way of creating; however, it is not the only way. Did you ever have something special occur in your life out of the blue? Maybe you were walking on a beach and you found the most wonderful artifact. Maybe you were hiking in the mountains and you found some sort of treasure. Maybe you were tearing down an old wall to do some construction and you found a bag of coins. Maybe you were walking down the street and you found a twenty dollar bill. Money and gifts can and do simply pop into your personal reality. So, how do we get them to turn up in a steady flow? We "open up" to the receptive energies. And how do we open up to the receptive energies? We allow ourselves to relax and to flow with what is occurring in our life.

If you do not relax and open to receive, you will still receive your weekly paycheck for work you have done. If you "open" to receive, you may receive unexpected bonuses and money from areas of your life that you would not "expect" to receive from. Once the flood gates open to allow energy into your personal reality, you will feel gifts large and small coming to you. Part of this will be the fact that you are now "aware" that you are opening to receive and so you will be watching for your gifts to arrive. Do not discount any gift – a smile from a stranger as you walk down the street. Often you make note of those who frown at you during your day, however, you barely notice anyone who smiles at you. Remember the smiles and thank yourself for generating them and for noticing them. Every small gift has the potential to turn into a much larger gift.

As you become aware of these little gifts, you give them power. You give everything you observe power simply by placing your focus on it. You then send energy to whatever you are focused on simply by giving it your attention. There is a saying, "You go where your focus goes." Focus on the good and the vibrant and the joyful and the healthy. Keep your focus where you want it. You do not wish pain and suffering so do not focus on pain and suffering. Focus on health and healing. If you see a sick puppy, do not get all wrapped up in how awful it is to be sick. Focus on the magic of healing and the possibility of complete recovery. Use this type of focus with people as well. You may even use this type of focus with the world that you live in. Do not focus on the worst outcome; always focus on the best outcome.

So, as you continue to open yourself to receive, you will be allowing your focus to move in the direction of a positive outcome for you. Isn't that the idea? Don't you want your attention on the outcome that you seek and not on the outcome you do not want? Don't you want your power, your energy, running into the possible reality that you most wish to receive? You may send energy with your *attention*. You are an energy producing machine. Watch where you direct your energy and remember that you run your energy through you (the cells in your body) first. You get what you send out, so try not to send out punishment and revenge and anger. If you do send out punishment, revenge and anger it is not bad, it is simply energy that will affect *you*.

You live in a world of energy and you are made up of energy. Energy is based on cause and effect. There is no good or bad here. It's all what you decide that it is. No right way or wrong way. No God who punishes in the end. It is all simply energy; wonderful creative energy. God is the energy of pure light. Pure light is unconditional love and acceptance. No matter who you are, no matter how you see life and the world; God is the part of you that is unconditional, and *aware* that nothing is wrong and everything is in divine order.

So, relax into the part of you that is unconditional love and acceptance, and you will be merging with your own God-self. There is a saying that "God's ways are not man's ways." Why not try it God's way? What do you have to lose? Oh, I see, you do not trust God and you do not believe that God wants only the best for you. Well if God is *in* you and experiences *through* you, don't you think that God wants *only* the best for you? The fear of a punishing God is deep and affects many of you on a very deep unconscious level. Maybe you did not grow up in a religious family being taught about how God punishes the bad for their deeds; however, the energy of thought behind this belief is strong and it is circling the planet you live on.

Know that God is unconditional love. Know that God lives *in* everything and is waiting to come forward. You have lived in a state of fear long enough and it is time to switch over to love and acceptance. You will know when you have made the switch because you will begin to see love everywhere you look.

The best way to create anything you wish for is to stand back and allow life to unfold before you. When you allow life to determine how you will receive and when you will receive, you are putting your trust in your own God-self. As you continue to trust your own God-self, you are telling the universe that you are "open" to receive God energy. God energy is carried within each and every one of you. You allow God to work through you when you are open to unconditional love. If your love is always conditional and depends upon the behavior of others, you will be judging and not loving.

Here is the trick to unconditional love. Unconditional love does not mean that you sit back and allow others to use and abuse your good nature. Unconditional love means that you "see" or "understand" that everything is simply the flow of energy at work, and none of what occurs is really personal to you. If you take it personally, you are saying that you own it. Do not take life or life experiences so personally. If you are told by a two-year-old that he hates you, do you take it personally or do you hold a grudge? No, I do not think that you would. Do you take it personally if a limb falls from a tree and damages your car? No, I don't think you would; however, the blame game has become so big that you may sue whoever owns the property the tree may be growing on.

I would like to see you move away from blame. Blame is causing you huge problems, and blame is making *you* into a victim just by your thoughts. When you constantly blame others for your life, you are unconsciously turning yourself into a victim. You are turning your power against you and you are turning your creations into punishments. Wherever you have blame you are making someone guilty of an act. So where does this energy of blame begin and end? It begins *in* you and it runs through every cell in your body, and it is sent out from you and circles the atmosphere, and it draws from the field of all possibilities to its sender. So, now you have blame running through your veins; and blame of course draws guilt, since blame is actually pointing a finger at and saying, "You are the guilty party." And so now we have guilt, which requires some type of punishment.

So, here you sit with blame and guilt *energy* running through your body and so you *receive* exactly what you have ordered from the field of all possibilities that you live in. It has nothing to do with right or wrong! It is simply energy that *you* send through *your body*! Please begin to see how you are putting yourself in a victim role by blaming others. Allow yourself to see clearly and allow yourself to understand energy. There are no bad guys in God's reality! It is all God's children playing and learning to use their power and their ability to create. Sure, some of you get off to a very rough start, but you will learn. God is guiding each individual, and each of God's children will wake up to their ability and to their godhood.

Until then I would like you to lighten up please! You do not have all the answers, and most of you do not even have some of the answers. It would really be a good idea for you to sit back and *allow* the God in you to come forward and work through you. When you allow God into your life (your conscious life), you are allowing the part of you that vibrates at the highest rate to come into your daily consciousness and work for you. Wouldn't it feel good to know that the part of you that *knows* what is going on will be in charge? Wouldn't it feel good to know that your own higher self, or God-self, is leading the way for you? Wouldn't it be a good idea to put the most conscious part of yourself in charge?

My pen's favorite saying right now is, "Live like a feather on the breath of God. Then your life is taken where it needs to go." Live your life as God (who is love and light) would live your life. Live your life to the very best of your ability. Do you find the best in fear and judgment and blame, or can you do a little better? I am not asking you to make huge changes here. I am simply suggesting that you allow the God in you to take over some of the time. You can still be in charge; just try to "let go and let God" at times also. You are God expressing in human form. How often do you allow God to express through you? What part of your life is being created by God (the conscious part of you) and what part of your life is being created by fear (the unconscious part of you)? You get to choose between love and fear every day and every minute of your life. Choose love! Choose God! Be free of fear and blame and judgment.

As you continue to discover your own self and how you create, you will learn how to un-create some of the problems in your life. You have created mountains out of mole hills in many cases and you are seeing problems where there are none. You are very good at fooling yourself and you are creating problems where none exist. Let go and allow God to assist you. Let go and *trust* that you are so much more powerful than you currently believe. You have God residing *in* you. You are the creative force of this universe and you are playing like you have no power at all....

As you continue your journey of self-discovery, I wish you to remember that you are the yin and the yang. You are both sides of everything and you contain all that is. You are the alpha and the omega, and you are the omnipotent one who is everlasting. You are only just now discovering your value and your uses. You are only just now discovering how magnificent you are and how powerful you are. You are just now beginning to wake up, and this awakening is a full-time job. It will take some time yet for this process to complete. Once the awakening of humanity is complete, life will look very different to you all. You will begin to see the love and the kindness that is right there inside of yourself, and inside of others. Right now you see kindness as boring, and you are totally unaware of what unconditional love looks like.

As you continue to see these energies come alive in yourself and in others, you will no longer find them so boring. You will lose your *need* for excitement and the zing you get from some of the denser energies. Right now you are thrill seekers and many of your thrilling adventures have caused problems for you. You frighten yourself often and you put yourself deeper into confusion and unconsciousness at every turn.

Once you come up out of unconsciousness, you will see how love and understanding are really the answers to your problems. Right now you simply put everything into two categories, and then you go along your merry way without a second thought. You choose to see life (and everything in it) as either good for you or bad for you. You see from "right" or "wrong" perspectives, and I would like you to begin to see through the eyes of love and understanding. You can actually start right here, right now, within your own self. Begin to see how you are programmed, by yourself and others, to behave in a certain way and to expect others to behave as you behave. But what if the others have not had your programming and your life experiences? What if their experience was less traumatic than yours? Wouldn't they then have less fear regarding certain situations than you might have, simply because of your programming and your mistrust of certain situations in life? And this is where we develop opposing views of reality; and this is how one side says, "This is right and good" while the other side stands in their fear and mistrust and fights back.

Mistrust is a very *big*, very *strong* energy. Mistrust will give way to love and understanding once *you* begin to let go of *your* need to be "right." I am talking to "you" right now – this you who is sitting here reading this book – not your husband or your wife or your neighbor – you!

So, as you learn to see life and the world through love and understanding, you will become a trusting person. Right now, if you are full of mistrust, that statement and that fact will feel dangerous to you. You feel that you need mistrust. Mistrust is your bedfellow, and you sleep with it and it feeds your addiction for you every day. And just what is your addiction? Your addiction is fear. You are fear addicted and you do not think you can live without fear. Many of you actually *believe* that fear is healthy. Fear is not so healthy as you now believe. Fear causes stress and constant pull on the adrenals in the body. Fear causes tension and upsets the nervous system. Fear is not bad! Fear is an emotion that is made up of very dense energy. This energy affects your mind and it affects your body and it affects how you deal with other individuals in life.

Let go of fear and come over to love. Get love addicted. Get on the love and understanding train and you will begin to enjoy this ride known as life!

⁂

As you continue to grow in trust you will be opening up the *receptive* channels *in* you. Reception is as important as giving out. What you give out you receive. What you are is what you get back from the universe. So, if you are full of fear and mistrust, you receive fear and mistrust. When you begin to shut down due to receiving fear and mistrust, you deplete your life of all the good things that you might *receive* if you only knew to send out good signals. Normally we would not use the term good, as it creates an opposite which is bad. However, since we are discussing all the good that you wish to draw into your life and personal reality, we will allow the word good to describe all energy. Everything is good and serves a purpose. Nothing is bad….

So, we have established our new reality as a good one and we will now let go of judging anything as bad. What does this do for us? Well, first off, you will stop fearing that the worst will happen in your life, and you will begin to feel like the best will happen and continue to occur in your daily life. You will know that any bumps along the way are just that, and you will learn to ride calmly through any turbulence in the energy field around you.

As you learn to stay calm through the turbulent times, with full knowledge that everything will work out and you are safe, you will be sending out signals that say, "I trust my life. I trust God the creator in me. I trust myself." Once we have you trusting yourself and knowing that you are doing well and creating the best for you, you will be letting go of all the judgment that you run through your body on a daily basis. When you stop running judgment through your system on a daily basis, your body will begin to relax. *You* will calm down even more and your body will respond by relaxing its muscles and its nervous system – no more tension, and no more back pain, and no more health problems caused by stress. You will be trusting you and this will allow you to open up and *receive*. When you send out calm, peaceful, loving signals into the field of all possibilities, you begin to receive all the wonderful things and situations that add greater calm, peace and love to your life.

Do you want a calm, peaceful, loving life? Let go and begin to see life through the eyes of trust. I know this idea frightens you to your core. Please give it a try. Trust will draw so much good into your daily life, and the results on a health level will be remarkable.

You do not realize the power and depth of your thoughts and your beliefs. You do not realize that you are creative by nature. You do not realize that you *control* it all by the energy that you create and send through your body. I have repeated this, in as many ways as I possibly can, just to get through the judgmental part of you to the unconscious part of you. We are trying to wake you up here. We are trying to show you how no one is to blame and everyone is walking around creating blindly. You are God creating in the material world. Look at your neighbor, he/she is God creating in the material world and is as blind to this fact as you are.

It is time to wake up and to learn how you create, and to begin to draw to you the energies that support you in life. Trust will support you. Fear and worry will wear you down. Be free of fear by moving over to trust and love. These two energies will open you up to acceptance. You then move into gratitude which keeps it all flowing. The more you are grateful, the more you will receive.

It doesn't matter what you are grateful for. Gratitude keeps you open and receptive. You can't show gratitude if you are in a constant state of mistrust. At some point you must begin to trust the flow of your life. Your life is energy in movement, and the more you trust your life the more energy you allow into you. The more you allow in, the greater gifts you might receive. Do you want health? Do you want wealth? Do you want love? It is all the same energy. You receive what you carry within you. If you carry positive energy you will continue to receive positive gifts. If you carry negative energy you will receive negative gifts.

So, change your perspective if you wish to change what you are receiving. Allow yourself to go with the flow of your life until you can reprogram yourself enough to come over to trust. Once you are trusting, you will have dropped your need, or desire, for judgment and control. Once you drop your need for judgment, you will allow room for peace and love and acceptance. All war begins with fear and judgment; even the war that rages within you. If you are at odds within your own self you will draw conflicting energies to you. When you let go of self-judgment and self-criticism you will no longer draw conflict into your personal reality. You will draw love when you begin to love and accept "you" unconditionally.

You will also draw love when you begin to love all of life unconditionally. This will, of course, fall into place once you are loving "you." The love of you is essential, and the only thing blocking love is fear. Fear then turns into judgment and criticism and anger and hatred, and just simply non-acceptance. So begin to love and *accept* you, and your life will soon be filled with love and acceptance. Why? Simply because you are a magnet and you draw to you that which you already are. Fill "you" up with love and acceptance and you will draw more of you to you.

You will begin to understand how you create your own personal reality at a much deeper level as you experiment with your daily lives. Try to see how it feels to not judge a single situation that occurs during your daily activities. No, "Oh no! Why did I do that?" and no name-calling and no self-criticism. Let go of everything except glorious self-acceptance and see how you feel at the end of your day. Do not judge anyone you come into contact with and do not judge how anything looks or feels to you. If you stub your big toe simply know that it will heal and you did not hurt you on purpose – or did you? There is a part of you that may carry guilt, and guilt will always draw some type of punishment to it. You will find that if you carry a lot of guilt, you may have been punishing yourself over the years without knowing (on a conscious level) that you have.

Let's say you were physically abused as a child each time you went against your parents wishes; you may have turned this into a kind of chastising where you began (as a small child) to believe that you were inherently bad or a problem for your parents. If you took on the role of self-chastising, you may carry a large *charge* of self-guilt about being bad and *causing* your parents to abuse you. Often, very small children do not *see* that their parents are the problem and in the throes of anger. The child begins to *believe* that he/she is the problem, and the child inadvertently begins to carry guilt about being bad.

So, as the child grows into adulthood, where does this large guilt charge go? It is still *in* you, and you must now let go of your guilt in order to release the energy that draws self-punishment to you. How do you let go of this guilt that you carry? You begin to *see* it all differently. You begin to see your parents as human, with the same level of unconsciousness that you have. You begin to see yourself as innocent, and as unconscious and unaware of the fact that you have been judging "you." Now you can forgive you for these false charges and let go of any future blame and judgment.

I realize that you were not all physically abused as children, and I am simply using this example to show you one specific possible cause of guilt and self-criticism followed by harsh judgment, which draws to it some type of punishment. The punishment then overpowers the guilt by allowing you to feel like a victim, and hence the good guy in the situation. If you are constantly feeling like a victim of life and of the world, there is likely self-condemnation at the base of your problems.

So, try to go one full day without judging you, or anyone else in any way whatsoever, and see how it feels. Once you have established that you can go a full day, then I would like you to give yourself the gift of non-judgment at least one day a week. After you master one day a week add another day; and then, as you master the second day, I would like you to add another and another, until every day is a judgment free day. Some of you will need more time than others to accomplish this task. Some of you have deeper wounds and carry greater *charge* concerning guilt and judgment. If you were sexually abused you may have been led to *believe* that it was your fault. There is a great deal of shame and guilt involved with sexual abuse, simply because your sex lives on earth are scrutinized and judged by so many.

Those of you, who are raised in an emotionally charged environment, where there is no sexual or physical abuse, are often emotionally abusing your own self as a result. You may constantly judge yourself for carrying and exhibiting emotions of any kind. You try hard to completely shut down your emotional body, or you may go the opposite way and get emotionally out of control. Either way you are carrying your own load of guilt, and now you more than likely feel guilty every time you express an emotion. You too will feel better once you see your parents as children who are learning to understand emotional behavior, and are just as unconscious as you are.

The idea here is to see it all as energy. There are no good guys because there are no bad guys. Everything is energy and levels of awareness, which will eventually open up to conscious behavior for all the inhabitants of earth.

So, as you go about your day, I want to see you happy and care-free and nonjudgmental at every turn. Have a very nice day and please be nice to you, and to the others who are playing here in this world of matter.

You will begin to discover that you have been the cause of all your problems, and you will learn how to fix all your problems simply by changing "you." You are the beginning and the end of all that exists in your life. You may choose to see life in a whole new way, and this will allow you to live in a whole new life. I do not suggest that you are to *blame* for anything. You are simply a creative being and you are unaware of this fact. The more you can become *aware* of how you create, the greater your chances are of changing what you create. Everything is already alive and a possibility; and you are simply drawing these situations to you from the field of all possibilities.

If you are an individual who has felt punished and abused, you may have a difficult time coming out of your "poor me" thoughts and beliefs. It will be helpful for you to begin to believe that you are *strong* and not weak. When you continually use a "poor me" attitude you continually draw "poorness" or "impoverishment" from all the possibilities available. "Poor me" includes "Look what he/she did to me;" "Look how awful they are to me;" "Look how much I've suffered through this;" "Look what a mess my life is;" "Isn't it a shame how the world is?" And my personal favorite "Look how God has made me suffer."

"Poor me" will get you exactly that – "poor." So, if you wish to draw wealth and health and happiness, I highly suggest you switch to "That's okay!" Start with, "My life is okay;" "The world is okay;" "Life is going along just fine;" "Everything seems to be okay and moving right along." You do not have to get all airy-fairy and positive right away. Start where you are and allow the energy to gently turn in a whole new direction. Allow yourself to drink from a new pool of water. Allow yourself to see the best instead of the worst in all situations.

So, as you begin to let go of any feelings of "Poor me, I'm such a good person; why does this happen to me?" You will begin to draw a more conducive reality like, "Wow! Life has been pretty good to me, and I think I'll begin to appreciate all that I do have and no longer focus on anything else." This line of thinking will lead you in a much better direction than any "poor me" thinking might.

So, do not worry that you are the cause of any problems you see, because you are changing your problems into challenges that will be overcome and dealt with. There really are no problems if you do not create them by seeing them as such. Your biggest fear is probably illness and disease. Did you ever notice how certain individuals deal with their illness in a very powerful and healing way? Certain individuals simply say, "I will get through this and come out on top." Others simply fall apart at the first sign of any problem. Those who fall apart easily are afraid. They carry a great deal of fear and mistrust, so they do not easily "believe" that everything will be okay. I want you to get strong in your trust, so that you will *trust* that everything will be okay. In this way, you will draw to you an outcome that is "okay." After a time you will learn to *believe* that everything is really great, and then you will begin drawing to you outcomes that are great!

So, as you continue to trust that life will take good care of you, you will be sending out strong signals that draw to you a life that is well taken care of. You do not wish to send out signals that say, "Life does not support me," as you will be creating a life that is not supported. You want to create a good support system for yourself, and you want to *know* that you are loved and supported.

The interesting thing is that once you begin to believe in

trust and support, you will find yourself sending out this message to others. You all emit signals and you will begin to send signals that support your fellow man, instead of sending signals that tear down your fellow man. You are on the precipice of a great discovery, and this discovery is that once you heal "you" by raising your vibration, you are immediately healing the world. You will begin to send out a higher vibration, which ultimately affects the entire world of matter; not just humans, but all life on earth is directly affected by these higher vibrations.

So, if you wish to raise and support the life on earth, you may choose to do so. The more light vibration "you" put out, the greater support you are giving to the world you live in. So, as you go about your day, I would like you to send out trust and positive thoughts about how life supports you – do you hear a beautiful song or maybe a bird singing? Do you see beautiful colors? Do you have the *gift* of sight? Do you feel loved by God or by another? Do you love God or another? Do you walk without support? Can you run? Can you surf? Can you ski? Does life support you with air to breathe? Do you have water to drink? Do you have hands to build? Do you have lungs to breathe? Do you have a mind that functions?

You are supported by life in so many ways and you only focus on what you don't have. Do not judge your life by what you don't have. Allow life to become all that it can be. Allow life to show you how you are loved and supported by allowing life to unfold before you. Trust life enough to allow life to do its job. Life is meant to be lived and enjoyed. Once you begin to trust life you will begin to see and to "enjoy" the gifts of your life.

So, as you move forward in your pursuit of happiness, try to raise your vibration and add a little love and kindness and gratitude and trust to your world, and everyone else's. Be of high hope and high optimism and higher thinking. Give love a chance and give fear a break by giving him a day or two off. You do not require fear to get you high, you do require love.

You are so afraid of everything, and it is time to become so in love with everything. Find a way to love and accept everything. Find a way to allow everything to unfold in your life. This way you are allowing it to change and to grow into something positive. I have given you the tools to work with. "What tools?" – you ask. The thoughts and ideas in this book will lift you up and allow you to see everything from a little higher perspective. I have repeated these examples for you often, in an effort to allow you to absorb them into your unconscious mind. Your conscious mind rejects and repels new ideas because it does not trust. The more I repeat a lesson for you the greater chance you have of *receiving* it.

So, as we close this book I wish to thank you for taking the time to read these words. Every little bit helps in the waking up process and every little bit makes a difference. I wish you well on your journey to perfect health, wealth and happiness. I know that you will do well with your search for enlightenment. You have opened a great deal just by wishing to know more, and to understand at a higher level. You are the light of the world and you are turning yourself on and beginning to shine brightly. You are the answer to all the questions. You contain all the information right inside of you. Get to know you better. You are God – the creator of your personal reality – and you can assist the world by assisting your own self.

When you get down and feel like your energy is pulling you down, the best thing you can do is something loving for yourself. Give yourself time to heal and give yourself a break from fear and judgment. Love yourself whenever and wherever possible. Self-love will heal you and lift you up. It is "all" within you, you will be sending out love simply by your act of loving you.

So, please pick up this book to reread whenever you feel

yourself forgetting the insights written here. We have other books to write, but, for now, I am going to give Liane a much-needed break. She will be happy to continue to be my pen and she looks forward to receiving more information in the future.

Go out into your personal reality and make it shine by allowing you to shine!

God

Introduction to
The Loving Light Books Series

There are many ways to go within to your core or your heart center. When you reach deep within your own psyche you will enter the core of your being. This is where soul and spirit resides.

For those of you who wish to reconnect with your own God-self I highly suggest that you read and reread the "Loving Light Books" series. This series is designed to draw you "within" to your own God-self and to allow you to peel away the layers that prevent you from becoming the loving, radiant being that you truly are.

This series of books was received by my pen (Liane) over a 10 year span of time and are quite remarkable. You will be led from an earthly way of viewing life to a more God-like way of viewing life. Everything is subjective in this three-dimensional world that you now call home. You, however, are a spiritual being and your life as a human is out of balance since you decided to enter matter. We will feed you information in this series that will allow you to *perceive* your current life in a whole new way.

These books were written for my channel and are most helpful to anyone who wishes to add more love and understanding to their life here on earth. If you are happy with where your life stands now, I do wish you well. If, on the other hand, you would like to learn more about your own spirit essence and how to connect with the part of you that draws love and unconditional light into your life, I highly suggest you begin your journey *within* by reading these helpful books.

I wish you well on your journey to discovering "you"....

God

Loving Light Books

Book 1: God Spoke through Me to Tell You to Speak to Him
Book 2&3: No One Will Listen to God & You are God
Book 4: The Sun and Beyond
Book 5: The Neverending Love of God
Book 6: The Survival of Love
Book 7: We All Go Together
Book 8: God's Imagination
Book 9: Forever God
Book 10: See the Light
Book 11: Your Life as God
Book 12: God Lives
Book 13: The Realization of Creation
Book 14: Illumination
Book 15: I Touched God
Book 16: I and God are One
Book 17: We All Walk Together
Book 18: Love Conquers All
Book 19: Come to the Light of Love
Book 20: The Grace is Ours

Also by Liane Rich

The Book of Love (Includes: For the Love of God)
For the Love of God: An Introduction to God
For the Love of Money: Creating Your Personal Reality
Your Individual Divinity: Existing in Parallel Realities
For the Love of Life on Earth
Your Return to the Light of Love: a guidebook to spiritual awakening

"I create a reality filled with love, joy, health and abundance!"

God's Pen

I first heard the voice of God in 1988. I was sitting in my back yard reading a book when this big booming voice interrupted with, "I am God and I will not come to you by any other name." I felt like the voice was everywhere – inside of me as well as in the sky around me. I was so frightened that I ran in my bedroom to hide.

This was not the first time that I heard voices. I had been communicating with my own spirit guide or soul for about a year. I guess my depth of fear regarding God, and all that he represented to me at the time, was just too much.

I spent two days trying to avoid the voice of God, which was patiently waiting for me to respond. By the second day I was exhausted from lack of sleep and decided to give in and talk with him. This turned out to be the greatest gift and best decision of my life.

In the beginning the voice of God would wake me in the middle of the night and tell me it was time to write. He said I had promised to do this work (I assumed he was talking about the soul/spirit me). I would drag myself up to a sitting position and watch in amazement as my hand flew across the page, while I tried to keep up by reading what was being written.

It was always so much fun to wake up the next morning and grab my notebook to see what God had written during the night. After some time the voice stopped waking me and I became comfortable picking up my pen and writing for God first thing in the morning. I think in the beginning I had to be awakened while still semi-conscious from sleep so I wouldn't object too much to the information that was being channeled through me.

As I grew less and less afraid (and more trusting) of God, he was able to communicate greater information. Some of the information is quit controversial, but I felt it important to just let it be and not censor it. I present the writings in this book to you as they were given to me.

For privacy reasons I am using a pen name. I asked God for a good pen name and he guided me to Liane which (I was told) in Hebrew means "God has answered."

At one point I became a little concerned about my sanity in all this, so I went to a hypnotherapist to find out what I was doing. Under hypnosis I saw this incredibly huge beam of light with a voice coming from within it. It was a giant "loving light" and felt so comforting and kind. It felt like that's where I came from. After that I stopped worrying about my sanity. If this is crazy, I think it's a very good kind of crazy to be....

In loving light, Liane

Loving Light Books

Available at:
Loving Light Books: www.lovinglightbooks.com
Amazon: www.amazon.com
Barnes & Noble: www.barnesandnoble.com

Also available on request at local bookstores

www.ingramcontent.com/pod-product-compliance
Lightning Source LLC
LaVergne TN
LVHW011420080426
835512LV00005B/163